WIN THE YOUTH SPORTS GAME

Praise for *Win The Youth Sports Game*

"*Win The Youth Sports Game* is a must-read for every parent who finds themselves caught in the grasp of the "youth-sport industrial complex." John nails the challenges, joys, and obstacles that young athletes and their parents face as they climb the competitive ladder. Whether your athlete is two years old, eighteen years old, or somewhere in between, you will learn about the road you are traveling and how to navigate it to a positive and healthy destination." —Jim Taylor, PhD, author of *Raising Young Athletes: Parenting Your Children to Victory in Sports and Life*.

"John Yeigh gives a unique perspective of the youth-sports journey. Keeping the big picture of the real value of youth sports in mind, he covers 54 obstacles and challenges that young athletes must overcome on their journey. This is eye-opening for parents and coaches alike and is not meant to discourage parents from embarking on the journey with their kids, but to prepare them for the road ahead. This is an important resource for parents because, although nothing fully prepares a parent for the youth-sports journey, they will have a clearer picture of what to expect and ultimately make the experience better." —Janis Meredith, author of *11 Habits of Happy and Positive Sports Parents*, and coach for sports parents.

"I love seeing parents think deeply about how to improve children's athletic experience. *Win The Youth Sports Game* is a valuable contribution to the ongoing conversation about healthy, positive participation in sports." —Angie Abdou, author of *Home Ice: Reflections of a Reluctant Hockey Mom*.

"I love how John takes the reader on a journey from youth to college sequentially—what a cool concept. He has given a must-open gift to parents and coaches who want better for their kids. If you are currently in the 'muck' of everyday youth sports, this book will help you get above the mess, so that you can clearly see how to help your athlete thrive in a youth sports world where most are frustrated and burnt out." —Andrew Simpson, author of *The Youth Truth: Coaching & Parenting in Today's Crazy Youth Sports World*, and performance and mindset coach.

"When a kindred spirit takes an enormous amount of time and energy to get out the truth about youth sports, I'm all for it. The book is spot-on for parents to help their athletes. All of it." —Steve Morris, author of *What Size Balls Do I Need?*, soccer coach, and youth-sports advocate.

"As any parent of a young athlete quickly discovers, youth sports can be a complex and treacherous maze, where good intentions can often get lost in all the competitiveness. John Yeigh's new book is an invaluable guide to navigate this world, written with real insight and perspective by a parent who knows all the ropes. I'd have given a lot to have read it before my own kids started sports!" —W. D. Wetherell, author of *Soccer Dad*.

"John Yeigh thoroughly addresses the issues confronting successful outcomes for children and sports. The youth sports conflicts are at a boiling point for American children, their families, and schools—and John has identified 54 obstacles we adults must work to recognize and overcome. His is a must-read for those of us involved with children and sport." —John E. Tufte, EdD, author of *Crazy-Proofing High School Sports*.

"Navigating the modern youth-sports journey can be taxing and expensive. *Win The Youth Sports Game* does a phenomenal job of highlighting the challenges and guiding the necessary steps specific to a player's needs." —Mike Just, author of *Just Baseball*, coach and former professional.

WIN THE YOUTH SPORTS GAME

HOW ORDINARY KIDS CAN THRIVE

JOHN YEIGH

Skyhorse Publishing

10 9 8 7 6 5 4 3 2 1

Library of Congress Cataloging-in-Publication Data is available on file.

Cover design by Brian Peterson

Print ISBN: 978-1-5107-6345-6
Ebook ISBN: 978-1-68358-431-5

Printed in the United States of America

Dedication

This book is dedicated to all sports moms and dads who make the journeys possible, the coaches who enrich their athletes' personal development, and most especially, Megan and Evan, who shared their journeys with me.

Table of Contents

Acknowledgments

First and foremost, my thanks to Evan and Megan, who shared their challenging and successful sports journeys with me. Special kudos to soccer mom extraordinaire Karen, who did the heavy lifting in managing our kids' relentless youth-sports pursuits. Karen was also a supportive writing widow and proofreader throughout my authorship journey.

A hearty thanks to all the coaches, organizers, and volunteers that contribute to youth sports and the resultant positive development of kids. The following coaches deserve a direct honorable mention for their service to youth sports in general and Evan in particular: Jeff, Larry, Peter, Milko, John, Roger, Oscar, Doug, Tim, Kenny, K, Nate, Mike M, Tom P, Jason, Ryan B, Tom F, Ben O, Gary, Frank, Mike B, Ian, Dafydd, Darren, Eddie, Mastro, Ryan P, Stimmo, Paul, Darrin, and Pat. Special kudos to Coach Kenny who was an unpaid volunteer coach for seven years. Coaches Kenny and K, plus team manager Mike, also did a tremendous job of managing seven years of complex travel-team logistics.

I sincerely appreciate the help of my supportive editors Anne Cherry, Jessica Moreland, and Elizabeth Zack. I also want to thank my editors at Skyhorse Publishing: Jay Cassell, Kirsten Dalley, and Jennifer L.S. Pearsall.

Finally, my thanks to illustrator Timna Green and photographer Carolyn Kobosko.

Prologue

The 5,854-Day Journey Begins

When our family moved to England from the U.S. in 2001, our seven-year-old daughter, Megan, was fast and athletic. In soccer-crazed England, not only do athletic kids play soccer, *every* kid plays soccer. There are no exceptions. And, so, like all expatriates from the states, we immediately signed up Megan to play for her school team.

Upon arriving in England, I knew nothing about soccer other than it used a round ball. We did not have recreational or high school soccer when I grew up, and our family was fully invested in gridiron football. In fact, I had never even watched a soccer game, either live or on TV.

To kick things off, we bought our daughter the proper soccer "kit" which, when translated into American, means everything needed to play soccer. Her British coach provided a "kit list" that included a uniform, shin guards, a ball, and, of course, soccer "boots." I thought soccer players wore cleats, but due to all the rain, perhaps English players required special footwear. Also, who knew that seven-year-olds used a size 3 ball but graduated to a size 4 upon turning eight?

My wife, Karen, and I religiously attended Megan's games with her two-year-old brother, Evan, in tow. While Megan's athleticism provided a few moments of success, even I could tell that her foot skills and control were sorely lacking. Problem-solving and engineering father that I am, I just had to tinker with and fix these obvious constraints to her success. So, Megan and I practiced, redundantly, kicking the ball back and forth, back and forth. It didn't help.

I realized it was time to really learn about soccer, because, in England, soccer is everywhere. It's on the telly and in the newspaper dailies, and it's played continuously in every town park. If I was going to help Megan get better at the game, I needed to know more.

My investment in the sport wasn't enough. Megan just wasn't that into it. Her brother, still a toddler, was different. He often focused on kicking Megan's outgrown size 3 ball while circling the sidelines at her games. Slide tackling in the abundant English mud provided him more moments of sheer joy. He especially loved halftimes, where he got to shoot at the big kids' goals with the other tykes.

After three years and a subsequent job transfer, Megan happily hung up her soccer boots and successfully moved on to sports involving water rather than dirt. What does this mean to this book? It means the real story starts with our chubby, wellie-booted toddler named Evan.

While he started playing in the mud at his sister's games, Evan's dedication to sports took a path we could not have foreseen. Evan's U.S. journey in youth sports ultimately involved 719 games, 51 leagues, 76 tournaments, and 44 camps (far, *far* too many camps!). It ended, after 5,854 days, on a 130-degree, frying-pan-hot field in

New Jersey in July 2018. While Evan's journey was hugely rewarding, he and his cohorts encountered plenty of the typical sports-establishment challenges and obstacles. As I traveled the road alongside him, I discovered that these obstacles were the constant and overriding theme that transcends all youth sports—not just soccer. But in reflecting on all that I'd learned, I also realized that most of these challenges were *adult*-imposed!

This book follows the typical youth-sports development path from ages two to eighteen. This chronology is intertwined with alternating chapters that juxtapose a variety of sometimes outrageous obstacles that the athletes encounter and alternative paths to consider in remedy. The resultant approaches we took, both good and bad, provide an ongoing set of "lessons learned."

I've identified fifty-four challenges Evan and his peers faced along the way. They are highlighted with this roadblock sign [==] within the storylines and summarized in Appendix II for easy recall. Managing and overcoming these hurdles are key to any athlete's longer-term success in youth sports—and in many respects, they are the real story here.

I sincerely hope that the parents, coaches, and other mentors reading this book will, when the last page is turned, be better able to identify the obstacles to success common to all sports. With that knowledge in hand, you will be better equipped to help your athletes navigate their journeys through high school sports and, for some, college athletic programs. Most importantly, though, it will go a long way towards ensuring your children are thoroughly enjoying the ride. It should always and only be about the athlete's journey, to ensure in the end, that the game is won.

Chapter 1

Peewee Sports—A Perfect Place to Start (U5-U6)

During my three years of indoctrination in the ways of English soccer, I just did not "get it." I could not fathom why three billion people incessantly watched this boring sport and wondered why in the world they called it "the beautiful game."

Parking the Bus

Over the English Premier League's (EPL) history and the last thirty years of World Cups, the average combined score is a miserly two-and-a-half goals per game. This breaks down to roughly one-and-a-half goals for the winners and one for the losers, so, statistically, only about a half-goal difference.

The main benefit of these close scores is that the losing team always has a chance of catching up and, maybe, even winning. What fan doesn't jump out of their seat when, in the closing minutes of the game, their team pulls off an amazing score, such as one the New England Patriots made in the 2017 Super Bowl, or survives a defensive stop such as the one those same Patriots managed in the 2015 Super Bowl? Those heart-clutching, game-changing moments aside, sports can quickly become bore-fests when the leading team switches to playing only defense in the closing minutes to run out the clock. This happens in basketball, football, hockey, field hockey, lacrosse, and, especially, soccer. It's a smart strategy for coaches, one that helps ensure wins and lines the pockets of players and owners, but it's not a lot of fun for spectators. It's also not a lot of fun for young kids getting started in sports.

Soccer actually has a term for playing out games defensively: "parking the bus." Parking the bus is most commonly associated with coach Jose Mourinho, who successfully deployed this tactic during his tenures with the Chelsea and Manchester United professional teams. In reality, undertaking a defensive-focused strategy has probably been around since cave dwellers kicked coconuts between trees. That's fine for professional sports, but when it comes to parents managing the challenges of youth sport journeys with their kids, they need to ensure *they* don't simply park the bus. Kid athletes encounter many decision points throughout their journeys where direct parental support is needed.

I still had zero affinity for soccer and its mostly defensive approach when, in 2004, we moved from one luscious and beautifully green, soccer-crazed country to another. A job transfer took us from England to Singapore. While Singapore and Asia are about as culturally different as possible from England and Europe, the English Premier League still dominated sports interests and workplace discussions. Singapore even had a dedicated Manchester United store located just two blocks from our apartment.

In seeing that store, I finally began to understand the scale of this global soccer "thing." It was also clear that the branding efforts of Manchester United (and FIFA) were undeniably successful. International recognition of Wayne Rooney and Cristiano

Ronaldo, both of whom played for Manchester United at the time, easily trumped that of many popular U.S. athletes such as Peyton Manning, Alex Rodriguez, or Shaquille O'Neal. It seemed only Tiger Woods and Michael Jordan commanded the same kind of fan fervor that the global soccer stars did.

My daughter, Megan, never did come to love the sport during our time in England. She was particularly uninspired by the sport's parking-the-bus approach, and happily used our transfer to Singapore to hang up her boots.

That's the Way the Ball Bounces

My son, Evan, was a different case. He'd begun organized soccer at the age of four or "U5" via a program sponsored by his Overseas Family School in Singapore (the "U" is commonly used youth-sports jargon which refers to "Under or equal to" a certain age limit to ensure kids only have to compete against peers of equivalent age. For example, the U12 age group for the 2021–22 season could include all kids born in 2010 or later—in other words, they are age 12 or younger. Note that the birthdate and sport-season cutoff dates vary widely by sport/organization—more discussion to follow on age-related issues). He was the lone Yank in his international school class, where baseball, softball, and gridiron football were not to be found. The school was already chock-full of little soccer players.

His coach was a wild Australian with a mohawk haircut, and his teammates hailed from Australia, Japan, Korea, China, Thailand, the Philippines, India, New Zealand, the United Kingdom, and Singapore. I have never heard so many different accents trying to express "Kick me the ball!" either in their native tongue or a rendition of the local dialect familiarly termed as "Singlish."

As much fun as the kids had in this play, I still wondered at the sport's "beautiful game" moniker. The phrase origins are often attributed to soccer great Pelé, from his autobiography *My Life and the Beautiful Game*. Regardless of origins, it's abundantly clear this is a widely used phrase by fans of the sport and its fluid movements.

These peewee soccer games Evan participated in were meant to be the earliest expressions of "the beautiful game"—*not!* U5 soccer play involves dense masses of dark matter orbiting around the soccer ball nucleus. *All* the kids move about in one cohesive rugby scrum, trying to kick the ball and, often, the other kids' shins until they turn black and blue. Any peewee sport that uses a ball or puck—lacrosse, basketball, ice hockey, field hockey, football, and the like—is similarly congested and chaotic.

Peewee soccer is without organized plays and has no passing approach, scorekeeping, offsides, or goalkeepers. The only exception to the latter is with the occasional jerk of a coach who parks their team's biggest kid right in front of the miniature goals to act as a de facto goalkeeper. This defeats the entire purpose of getting little kids to run around the field. Purists sometimes lament the complete lack of structure in tyke soccer, as it evokes the epitome of parking the bus—the whole team acts as a defensive wall—but it eliminates undue pressure on the kids and keeps fun in focus.

On those occasions when the ball happens to supernova out of the scrum's orbit, the teams dash forward in classic kick-and-chase mode. Breakaways are led by the fastest kids, with the slower kids like Evan trailing behind like the tail of a comet. The breakaway ends when either a new circle of dark matter reforms around the ball or the biggest, fastest kid kicks the ball out of bounds. Scoring is as random as in the professional game.

"Bunch ball" provides lots of funny tyke moments of missing the kick all together, balls kicked the wrong direction, balls bouncing every which way, wrong-side goals aplenty, and kids tumbling down like Jenga blocks. Peewee soccer is tremendous fun for the kids and hilarious to watch. It also turns out that soccer is a typical first sport for tykes, along with swimming, gymnastics, dance, and martial arts. Other sports are too complicated (football) or require more advanced physicality (volleyball or basketball) for this age range.

For our family, bunch ball provided far more action than the peewee swim meets we attended. Swim meets consume a whole day to watch maybe two total minutes of action. Likewise, watching sports with kids of this age group easily beats those elementary school, chalk-on-blackboard music recitals. At least in soccer, kids get a chance to run around like maniacs, chase each other, and kick a ball all over the place.

Peewee bunch-ball is always chaotic, yet fun.

The best part about peewee soccer? *Every* kid left the field with a huge grin, regardless of win, loss, or scraped knee. I didn't yet "get" soccer, but, like most tyke sport activities, it provided many positive benefits—exercise, camaraderie, game playing, and lots of smiles. In hindsight, these were unknowingly our first baby steps on what was to become an extended family journey full of benefits and unknowing challenges in the world of youth sports.

Chapter 2

Select Sports: They Start Earlier than You Think (U7-U9)

Evan left international soccer behind, along with his strong British accent, in 2006, when my job posting returned our family to the U.S. We signed up Evan to play soccer in the local Annapolis, Maryland, recreational league in the spring of 2007.

He was assigned to the U7 Tigers, ably led by Coach Jeff. This was our first experience with weekly practices and an extracurricular team. The Tigers compiled a 3–2–1 winning record as spring thunderstorms limited the games. Evan enjoyed his first taste of organized sports, but anything involving six- and seven-year-olds should hardly be called "organized." Every kid we saw in this age bracket was happy just playing a sport, and Karen and I relished the action despite having no idea the long and complicated journey we'd begun.

Early Draft Choices

Evan continued with recreational soccer in the fall of 2007. At that point, Karen and I hadn't given any thought to considering other sports, let alone the implications of continued involvement in youth athletics, but this is the period when parents should be doing just that. In my naïve expectations, I believed such issues were readily addressed sometime in the teenage years. I had no inkling that the foundation for a host of future travel-team parental anxieties was being laid with seven-year-olds like Evan. In many cases, the trajectory of a child's sports journey was effectively cemented during these formative years. I later learned that the initial decision point for long-term sports activities is more likely nearer to age eight.

Evan was assigned to Coach Peter and the U8 Black Knights. The kids, for the first time, received a uniform of sorts, as each team was assigned to wear a colored Hanes Beefy-T cotton shirt. (The time for Adidas, Nike, and Under Armour tech gear would come later.) Evan's team was allocated the color black, hence the inspiration for the Black Knights' name. The team finished the regular season a respectable 3–3–1—and, wait for it—was now in the playoffs!

The Black Knights won its initial playoff game and qualified for the championship game. In the finals, the black T-shirts would be facing the undefeated red T-shirts, named something like the Red Devils or Red Raiders.

The Reds had dominated all opponents through the regular season, including the Black Knights. Naïve me had no idea, before that fateful playoff day, that the Reds were already a well-established *select* team.

Long before our return to the U.S., the Red's Coach Chris had become active within the local organization in order to recruit the best and most athletic Annapolis-area kids. In addition, the parents of his players actively recruited the strongest athletes from their respective elementary schools to further bolster the Red's team's strength. Its twelve-player roster was *stacked*.

The championship game was a classic David versus Goliath, with the good-guys wearing black. In addition to being out-talented, the Black Knights were also outmanned, with just nine players for the championship game. However, the team did have five things going for it: First, midfielder Owen had more speed and energy than any Red-team player. Second, striker Julio was by far the most talented U8 player but had been overlooked by the Reds, as he hadn't come from their recruiting neighborhoods. Third, disciplined Evan flawlessly stayed on defense acting as the designated "sweeper," and fourth, the Knights had a secret weapon, goalkeeper Carl, who wasn't fast or athletic but could catch well and was a head taller than any other kid in the league. Finally, and perhaps most important, the Black Knights played as a *cohesive* team rather than as a bunch of individual kids seeking stardom.

The game ended in a 1–1 tie during regulation time, and the game moved onward to penalty kicks. With Carl the Giant taking up half the peewee goal, the Reds didn't stand a chance.

Sucked In

Who knew that select sports started before age eight? (Note: this is the first appearance of my roadblock symbol—[==]—noted in the prologue and used to indicate one of 54 challenges I identified during Evan's youth-sports journey.) And who could imagine that adults stacking the deck, even with seven- and eight-year-olds, is no guarantee of victory? The Black Knights were surprising season champions, and Evan got his first joyous taste of sports success and a trophy. He may even owe his long-term sports affinity to Carl, who was clearly the Black Knights' MVP, rather than the athletic Julio or Owen, both of whom made it to college sports.

Either way, involving my eight-year-old in his first "organized" sport became both a sweet memory and a turning point in understanding the machinations of youth sports in general.

This was the first time that youth sports had revealed its many underlying interests and dealings that are managed by parents and organizers in the know. Naïve parents like Karen and me just didn't know that the elite youth-sports train may have already left the station, nor that our kid wasn't on board. Fortunately, there was still time to catch the train at future stops by investigating potential shortcuts. Had I done a little research, I would have discovered that tryouts in a variety of sports (baseball, basketball, soccer, etc.) are widely advertised for kids beginning around age seven (U7-8). Team *rankings*, surprisingly begin with children as young as age five for baseball and eight to ten for other sports. The major youth football and cheer organizations even sponsor national championships for kids as young as eight.

We also quickly discovered that being sports parents involved much more than just showing up for games. Our introduction to parental volunteering was to provide the peewees with halftime and after-game snacks and drinks that fostered an energy boost, as well as the initial stages of sports-team camaraderie. These friendly rituals would continue until more serious travel sports began around age eleven.

The progressive parents always provided healthy apples, oranges, Gatorade, and water, which were eagerly consumed. A few naughty parents supplied fatty chips and sugary juice boxes that the kids devoured with equal gusto. Drinks and snacks with team buddies always generated postgame smiles. The game's outcome didn't seem to matter much to the kids—but winning was clearly a growing focus for a number of parents.

In the spring of 2008, Evan was assigned to the U8 Hurricanes rec league team with Coach Larry. Evan became the full-time sweeper or primary central defender. This positional assignment was due to his defensive discipline and tenacity. It certainly wasn't due to exceptional athleticism, but very few eight-year-olds have the ability to remain vigilant on defense, as the bunch ball mentality still prevails. I suspect Evan's remarkable focus here may have resulted as much from a physical inability to run for the whole game as for innate self-control.

Evan was beginning to enjoy the entire sports experience and asked us to buy a soccer net and plastic dribbling cones for home use. These allowed him to mimic skills and activities he learned at practices. After games and on nights without scheduled team practice sessions, Evan started practicing with me and making runs toward the goal in our narrow side yard, just for the fun of it. "First to ten goals wins!" over and over and over again. At age eight, this was the start of both Evan's never-ending supplemental training and my increasing involvement in his athletic pursuits.

> "First, master the fundamentals." —Larry Bird, three-time NBA champion and league MVP

Joining the Hurricanes marked an important turning point in Evan's attitude about playing. He was beginning to genuinely love everything about the season: teammates, practices, games, the coach, extra practices with me—*everything*. And, he just wasn't satisfied with the limited fall and spring recreation leagues. He wanted and asked for more.

I stepped up to the plate and started managing tournaments to provide supplemental play beyond the leagues for Evan and his buddies. Coach Dad still had never played one minute of soccer, but by this point, I had developed a basic understanding, and even a bit of joy, about the sport. In truth, I was slowly getting sucked in, despite soccer being a sport inherently outside my wheelhouse. Over the next few years, I managed and coached seven tournaments, of which the team won one and was a runner-up twice.

In the fall of 2008, the local rec league organization started to sort players and assign teams to levels for the U9 players. To this day, I have no idea what the criteria for selections were, as no tryouts or evaluations were held. Evan landed on the U9 Dragons, assigned to play in the county's Division 2, one of six such divisions. The parents of the "Reds," now ascending to the same U9 age bracket were already making space on their boys' trophy shelves for their anticipated cruise through Division 1.

The U9 Dragons, led by the soccer-competent Coach Milko, magically clicked as a team and went 9–0 for the season. With Evan playing defensive sweeper, the team gave up just four goals all season, the lowest goals against average in the entire county, including all age groups U6-U18 across all divisions. It was, literally, the best defensive result among hundreds of teams. I not only enjoyed this season but was also particularly proud of the team's cohesive efforts, which bagged Evan's second league championship in a year. Oh, and about those Reds? I can happily report their trophy shelves still have one vacant space collecting dust.

Sports in this preteen, pre-travel team era encompass the most joyous and innocent times for kids regardless the sport in which they participate. The issues concerning playing time, tryouts, competitiveness, over-coaching and yelling, divisions and ranking, high costs, and overzealous adults had not yet arrived. Kids ran around, had a blast, played with their buddies, and improved their game. Some teams, of course, had some success, but winning wasn't critically important to the kids. They just wanted to play, and that's what they got to do.

At the same time, it had become clear that select sports had already begun in earnest, and travel sports were looming. Not only was this "soccer thing" starting to grow on me, I could see that, for Evan, sports were becoming a larger part of his life.

Chapter 3

Mama, Don't Let Your Kids Grow Up to Be Special

I played five sports as a kid, three sports through junior year in high school, and two sports into college. I still participate in a half dozen sporting activities and regularly change them up. Though I am now of social security age, I'm still not settled in my interests and activities. I enjoy kicking a ball, throwing a spiral, or shooting "H-O-R-S-E," especially when invited to participate with Evan and his buddies.

This is not the way with so many of today's child athletes.

Designated Hitter

Kids today become far more skilled and proficient at whatever their chosen activity is, whether it's sports, music, computer-gaming geekdom, or being the most outrageous black-fingernailed Goth they can imagine. Because of today's culture change that puts the focus on one activity, Evan and his teammates are far better soccer players than my generation was at all our sports combined.

But a zillion players are still far better than Evan and his buddies.

Today's child athletes become specialists at the earliest ages. Indeed, specialization can be a necessity in sports that require long-term finite and repetitive skills development such as soccer, golf, tennis, baseball, field hockey, volleyball, lacrosse, and the like (compared to sports that also require a maturing athletic development such as track, basketball, and football). Still, specialization is something that comes with unintended consequences [==].

Evan became defensive-oriented in his soccer playing at U8 and a specialized defensive (holding) midfielder almost exclusively since travel soccer began at U10 (age nine); the latter is the equivalent of a roving middle linebacker position. As a result, he moves well without the ball and is inherently good at field positioning. He can defensively win balls, control possession, and distribute (pass) balls well, but he cannot finish (score) for diddly. In fact, Evan will pass the ball to a striker (scorer) even when parked right in front of a wide-open net that's shouting at him, *Shoot!* To this day, Evan passes rather than shooting.

> "A good hockey player plays where the puck is. A great hockey player plays where the puck is going to be." —Wayne Gretzky, all-time leading NHL scorer

There are many books and websites that highlight the potential for repetitive injuries, burnout, and negative emotional issues with early specialization, but few highlight the potential long-term impact on the child's overall sports journey. Naïve parents like

Karen and I had no idea our kid's playing position was being set in concrete when he was only nine. The skill set needed for that position fit him, so, like most sports parents, we simply rolled with it. Nor did Karen and I give the specialization a thought regarding the potential implications for Evan's skills development, high school play, or college recruiting eight years later. Despite now having a fundamental understanding of the many specialization pitfalls, I'm not sure our path would have been much different; but for others, it might.

The Wrong Kind of Special

In truth, Evan had super-specialized in a common position. Think outfielders in baseball, linemen in football, halfbacks in field hockey, or setters in volleyball. When college recruiting began, we soon discovered midfielders outnumbered all other positions by a ratio of perhaps five to one. Can't score? Be a midfielder. Can't defend? Be a midfielder. Slow? Be a midfielder. Weak positioning skills? Be a midfielder. No discernable sports skill at all? Call yourself a midfielder or perhaps an outfielder, roleplayer, or sixth man. Having said they'd watched a few professional games on TV even seemed qualification enough.

The mass of high school midfielders creates huge issues for college recruiting. Skilled midfielders must somehow stand out, and college coaches must identify the most skilled midfielders from among those masses. The selection process is further muddied by the fact that the multitudes of midfielders receive, at most, 30 percent of the playing time versus other positions at college identification (ID) camps, soccer's equivalent to football combines or basketball AAU summer games.

At ID camps, any random group of twenty field players is typically comprised of three defenders, three strikers, and fourteen midfielders. Coaches sort the players into the commonly utilized

4-4-2 formation of four defenders, four midfielders, and two strikers. This means the fourteen midfielders have to share playing time for four positions, and end up playing maybe one-third of the time. This creates a *huge* obstacle for the midfielders when it comes to getting noticed by the college coaches.

Regardless of Evan's interest in any particular college, he attended ID camps to play soccer above all else. He would not tolerate waiting on the sidelines for a few minutes of playing time. He simply switched to defense, because unlike many midfielders, he could. Defenders were far fewer in number and often played every minute at camps.

Playing as a defender didn't help his cause for recruitment as a midfielder. Coaches cross-comparing Evan's camp application with observations about midfielders came up with a blank. Coaches just were not looking for him on defense, even though he had a couple of particularly strong camps playing at the defensive fullback position. Just one NCAA Division I (D1) coach specifically noted and acknowledged Evan's positioning versatility (see coaches' comments in Appendix III).

Early specialization can be devastating for kids starting out as goalkeepers, particularly in soccer (though also in other sports). In the peewee years, soccer nets are about four feet high (U6-U9), and later, six feet high (U10-U12), where goalkeepers of all heights can be effective. When nets move to eight feet in height (U12-U13), shorter keepers are at an enormous disadvantage. Just as in basketball or volleyball, height is a key attribute in goalkeepers.

Several height-challenged goalkeepers I knew flamed out once the game moved to the higher and wider nets. Their future journey in youth soccer was then further stymied because youth goalkeepers typically don't have the opportunity to develop the foot skills necessary to transition to field play successfully. Karen and I also knew a highly skilled goalkeeper who topped out at 5'6," following in the footprints of his petite parents. This keeper had excellent range, great hands, and a strong punt, but, in his mid-teens, playing time diminished in favor of players with broader wingspans. In fact, except for a few "sweeper keepers" like Germany's Manuel Neuer or Brazil's Ederson Santana de Moraes, most pro goalies don't have the foot skills of the field players. After all, goalkeepers spend most of their time catching rather than kicking.

Early partitioning of kids to specific positions is a reality of youth sports. But this specialization can inadvertently be the endgame for kids assigned to sports or positions that don't suit their likely physical traits (size, eyesight, coordination, pace) or match their underlying personality traits. Specialization can also lead to overuse injury or simply result in burnout [==].

> "Specialization is one of the most prevalent and disturbing trends in youth sports." —Bob Bigelow, former NBA player and leading youth sports advocate

Further, the competition for college slots is particularly tough for the ultra-specialized positions, such as goalkeepers. For instance, in soccer, the typical forty- to sixty-player ID camps would have anywhere from five to ten goalkeepers attending. When divided across fifteen- to twenty-player teams, each team would end up with two to four keepers who then had to split up game time; keepers were often lucky to get twenty minutes of playing time each hour. Goalkeepers have the further challenge of potentially being assigned to a camp team with either great defensive capabilities or against a team with no offensive capabilities, further compromising their ability to demonstrate their goaltending skills to college coaches.

Lost in the Shuffle

Even when goalkeepers do get a fair look from recruiters, the numbers still work against them. Each team needs just one starting goalkeeper every four years and one backup keeper, regardless the sport. A team with a solid sophomore or freshman doesn't need to recruit another goalkeeper for a couple of years. Backups can, effectively, be on the waiting list until their senior-year opportunity, only to be bumped by one of two new freshman recruits, as two replacement freshman goalkeepers will undoubtedly be recruited just in case the displaced senior quits.

Examples of challenges to goalkeepers abound. Evan's high school team had probably the second-best keeper in the county, but he played only occasionally during his secondary school career. This excellent athlete basically rode the bench in high school, even though he made it to a college team. Similarly, the high school's starting goalkeeper often rode the bench for his travel team behind a player who was also on the national team. In other words, highly skilled goalkeepers can end up in a situation where they mostly don't play.

These specialization problems occur in sports besides soccer. Players specializing in either the most common positions or performing basic activities will undoubtedly incur more of a challenge getting noticed by high school and college coaches. Coaches focus on basketball players that get the ball in the net, baseball players that hit, volleyball players that kill and block, and football players that get the ball down the field and across the goal line. A fantastic dribbler who can't score, a hitter who can't field, a setter who can't spike, and a tight end who can't catch are going to have more difficulty getting noticed even if they are the very best at every other aspect of their position.

Working the Niche

The odds of playing college sports are hugely increased in those disciplines having either moderate or minimal youth participation or bigger college rosters. Lacrosse, crew, and sometimes even baseball are good examples compared to the participation draw football and basketball receive. I read of a father who guided his two kids to excel in the javelin throw—a truly niche sports activity if ever there was one—but it helped his kids land Ivy League acceptances. Comparatively, obtaining a college roster spot in men's soccer is one of the more difficult, after men's basketball and women's volleyball. Knowing that, and had Evan's *main* objective been to play college sports (something he always claimed to want and even though he had no professional aspirations), he should have skipped soccer and considered an alternative sport. But soccer seemed to be coded into Evan's DNA, and he was always committed to the journey, specialization and all.

Chapter 4

Travel-Team Roulette, Shenanigans with Coaches, and the Rankings Game (U10-U12)

Following the fall U9 season, Evan still wanted to play more soccer. Nine-week seasons of two practices per week and nine forty-minute games (depending on rainouts) were just not enough soccer for him. In the U.S., soccer doesn't generate daily pickup games in every town park as we had experienced in England.

Youth soccer, like most modern youth sports, is only about organized teams and leagues. The widely deployed term *pay to play*, used in derision, comes into play here. In fact, today, very few kids play pickup games in any sport. This is a fundamental shift from the days of my youth, when we played sandlot games year-round in football (two-hand touch), basketball (H-O-R-S-E), baseball (pickle), kickball, and other energetic outdoor activities such as dodgeball, tag, red rover, freeze tag, red light/green light, etc.

Forward Progress

Since Maryland's outdoor sports go into winter hibernation for the younger age groups, I had to find alternatives to satisfy Evan's newfound passion. I started researching and luckily discovered an advertisement from a U10 travel-team coach who needed an extra player for winter indoor leagues, starting immediately.

Our Maryland region has four indoor warehouse sportplexes with artificial turf fields that are roughly half the size of regulation fields. The operators of these sportplexes sponsor indoor leagues typically in seven-versus-seven (seven members from each team on the field) format.

After email exchanges with the coach, Evan was instantly double-carded (added to this team's roster in addition to his regular team), playing up one older age group, and now also on the Red Storm travel team. These were all new aspects of youth sports for us.

Evan's travel-team journey was launching, albeit slowly. Each time he joined a new team, the coach initially utilized him on a limited basis. His physical movements on the field were just not athletically or aesthetically appealing, and his pace was a bit slow. Despite this, his net defensive play was just as effective as some of the more athletic looking players. He had good positioning, discipline, and a continuous hustle. As a consequence, he would often start off on the bench as a substitute, work his way toward starting roles, and then sometimes receive among the most playing time. This became a wash-rinse-repeat sequence with each new team or coach.

Travel soccer also ended multi-sport and well-roundedness for Evan at the young age of ten. He had been a solid local swimmer with a particularly strong butterfly stroke. He was also a top ten regional sailor, which was his sister's (collegiate top ten) and my primary sport. (Forevermore, our parental sports duties would be split into "surf 'n' turf," for her and him.) Evan also had many recurring opportunities to take up lacrosse, as Annapolis is a lacrosse-centric town. In addition to lacrosse, our city offers exceptionally strong swimming and sailing programs, with all three sports providing enhanced, longer-term athletic prospects for high school and college play. Despite a variety of excellent sport options, Evan was always happiest whenever he was lacing up his boots and running onto the pitch for practices or games. While I may have wished for another sailor, it wasn't to be.

Balls, Balls, Balls

During his tenth year, Evan started to become "one" with his balls. Wherever he went, he brought his soccer balls along with him. While he already had a couple, we needed to get more, many more—one for each car, one for the school and sports backpacks, one for the living room, one for his bedroom, and extras for practice. When Evan left the house, he took along a ball in case he could squeeze in juggling, dribbling, or off-the-wall kicking practice.

One curious source for extra balls came from scavenging for balls lost in the woods adjacent to playing fields. A couple of practice fields were located next to a thicket of prickly briar patches and a mosquito-infested swamp. Hidden troves of balls awaited any explorer who dared enter. Evan treasured these free balls, probably due to our risk to life and limb to extract them. The secret is now out as to why I wore jeans, long-sleeved shirts, and boots whenever games or practices were on fields next to thick woods. Over the years, we recovered perhaps five excellent-condition balls for his growing quiver, as well as many sun-rotted ball carcasses, zillions of lacrosse balls, a few baseballs and tennis balls, and even one decent football.

Evan's strong romance with his soccer balls lasted just a couple of years. As a preteen, it suddenly became uncool to be toting a ball around like a teddy bear. Coaches mostly managed his (practice) balls from that point forward.

Angling Up for More Playing Time

The new Red Storm team provided our first taste of the challenging realities of higher-level sports, as well as the commitment their travel involved. For example, Red Storm participated in a tournament in Gettysburg, Pennsylvania, where the team got crushed and handily lost all three games. (Some teams of ten-year-olds were already amazingly good, something you probably wouldn't think was possible at that age. Then again, pro player Christian Pulisic had grown up in the area, and I wouldn't have been surprised if he'd been among the attendees during that tournament.)

The Red Storm coach moved Evan to the holding midfielder position, his primary position for his final eight years. At ten years old, he wasn't speedy enough to play defense with kids one age group older, but holding midfielders don't have to be the fastest player on the pitch. Rather, they should be defensively disciplined, focused, and able to distribute the ball effectively, all attributes Evan possessed.

Evan continued to play on several Annapolis rec league teams and the Red Storm travel team throughout 2009–2010 (U9/U10 and U11/U12). We wondered if playing up an age group would eventually become an issue. Coach John assured us, "Kids can continue to play up as long as they are not bench sitters." That seemed an acceptable approach, but what Karen and I didn't see coming was the roster crash and player re-sorting coming at the kids as teams transitioned from eight-versus-eight play at U11 age to eleven-versus-eleven play at U12 or U13 ages (depending upon the league).

After the Fall 2010 season, Evan ended up in sports limbo, playing up on two U12 rec league teams (one age group older) but no travel teams. During this period, he was back to playing defensive center back/sweeper, and at a lower level of play. At the end of the season, one parent said about Evan, "When you look up the definition of 'sweeper,' there's a picture of Evan." Teammate Stevie described Evan's capabilities this way: "We don't have a defense. We just have Evan." Nice compliments, surely, but Evan was playing a bit below his abilities, and I was desperate to get him back to a more challenging program.

Try, Try Again

The path back to travel sports started in earnest after the Spring 2011 season when Evan was set to participate in a series of tryouts for several fall teams. I was worried, so worried, in fact, I Googled how to help kids get noticed during tryouts.

One website suggested the kids wear bright colors to stand out. This led me to what our family now calls "the magic fluorescent yellow socks." Wearing them, Evan truly stood out among the multitudes of boys competing for team placement. His legs screamed, *Watch me!*

The socks did the trick, but he refused to ever wear these socks again for practices or other tryouts. Clearly, conformity and peer pressure override a kid's desire to get noticed. To this day, Evan remains angry with me for making him wear those flamboyant socks even the one time. In fairness to me, other kids wore similarly loud gear, including neon pink and fluorescent green socks, a "fashion" trend I observed at many tryouts over the years. I do believe most of the offensively dressed players at these tryouts were selected—but, at the same time, the selections may have been a matter of skill over attire, as only the solid players had the guts to wear flamboyant clothing.

Bait and Switch

With these June 2011 tryouts for the coming fall season, we had targeted two teams for which Evan most wanted to play. One was a local rising U13 team (one age group older) with whom he was regularly practicing and playing in tournaments as a guest player. Another was a rising U12 travel team with whom he had guest practiced several times as a pre-tryout. The U13 team was transitioning from the local rec league to the Baltimore Beltway Soccer League (BBSL), which was a step up. The U12 team would be playing in the National Capital Soccer League (NCSL), a further step up from BBSL.

Both coaches indicated Evan was a sure selection, as they were already familiar with his abilities. Then each coach reneged and placed him on a new start-up "B team" within their organizations and with new coaches. The coaches offered similar excuses, identifying Evan as a stalwart talent around which these new B teams would be built.

In truth, these were nearly identical bait-and-switch maneuvers in which Evan and several other players were being manipulated to help these two coaches expand their organizational empires [==]. Either B team would have been a step backward for Evan. We said no thanks.

Evan was now a displaced athlete without a team, which greatly concerned us at the time. I have since come to learn that solid players will have options, as teams are constantly looking for decent players to replace others who move onward, get injured, drop out, or switch teams; much of youth sports turns out to be a game of attrition. While I did not want Evan to become a serial team-hopper, a sport parent's relentless objective during the journey is to find an appropriate fit with both team and coach [==]. In fact, maintaining the ideal level of team play and suitable coaching situation is probably the single most critical parental challenge throughout the youth-sports journey.

By the time the Fall 2011 season came around, we thought we'd found a good fit with another rising U12 select team, although the team did not travel. This team owned a coveted slot in NCSL, which was a definite step up. This team also had a few good players from the peewee Reds team of several years back, but also a bunch of weaker, fill-in players. The coach turned out to not be the best fit as well. While Evan appreciated the higher-level NCSL competition overall, he did not enjoy the team's disorganized play, which resulted in a weekly spanking.

The next stop in travel-team roulette was the Severna Park Fury team during the 2011–12 winter indoor season. Coach Kenny liked Evan's foot skills and defensive tenacity. The tryouts were on smaller indoor fields, which, fortunately, did not overemphasize Evan's mediocre pace (the other Fury players were all quite quick). Fury needed to add one reliable player to its fourteen-player roster (eight-versus-eight play) for the spring season, since several players would be regularly unavailable due to baseball commitments.

Evan became number 35 permanently. The number was not by choice or part of any team sequence, but rather the result of the Fury coach having one spare uniform numbered 35. Over the next seven years, Evan would receive many "You suck, 35" or worse banter, some "Settle down, 35." from referees, especially in the early years, and even a few "Great game, 35!" from opposing coaches and, notably, two sportsman-minded opponents. Evan was also, uniquely, the first Fury team member who did not live and grow up in the town of Severna Park, which was about twenty-five minutes from our Annapolis home. Thus, number 35 was an outsider due to his remote residency and out-of-range number.

In his first Severna Park Fury season, in the spring of 2012, the U12 team played in Division 5 of the NCSL and crushed it by going 10–0–0. Evan proved to be a key team member when Fury could muster only eight players (no available substitutes) for several games, due to the aforementioned conflicts with baseball schedules. But, in games when the Severna Park locals had no attendance conflicts, new recruit Evan was frequently demoted back to the bench despite contributing successfully in the tight and shorthanded games. Playing time is a constant issue in youth sports, which Evan was experiencing firsthand.

In addition to the NCSL league games, Fury played in its first two travel tournaments (Columbia, Maryland and McLean, Virginia) and won both. The McLean tournament was a huge win, as Fury beat several teams ranked much higher. Evan played well in this tournament but was on the bench when Fury conceded two goals. I had started to become far more observational concerning playing time and positioning, and I was making the effort to thoroughly document statistics, progress, and challenges the athletes encountered. We were now watching English Premier League (EPL) games (Go Liverpool!), attending occasional D.C. United games, and at least one U.S.-based exhibition game of European clubs (Manchester United, Barcelona, Chelsea, Liverpool, and Tottenham) each summer. I began regularly reading technical books on soccer and was really taking in the details as the team moved up to play at higher levels.

After nearly ten years, I was starting to "get it."

Getting to the Dance—the Rankings Hoopla

Youth sports also entered the digital age during this period, and team Fury was an early adopter. Fury maintained rosters, schedules, and the all-important pictures of the kids playing on the Shutterfly website. (To Shutterfly's credit, the site sustains the team account nearly a decade later, and we can still download pictures from this formative sports period.) Fury and Evan's other teams later switched and utilized the TeamSnap software system to host and manage team information and game videos. While TeamSnap worked great for us, I am sure the functionality and applications are ever-expanding and improving.

Today, there is a proliferation of team and player management software platforms, including Stacksports, RosterBot, HomeTeamsONLINE, SportsEngine, SportsSignUp, LeagueApps, Playmetrics, GameChanger, and more than thirty others. Many incorporate medical forms, liability releases, and health check (pandemic) applications. In addition, there are the companies that manage sports events, such as EliteTournaments, frequently used in our region, plus ActiveNetworks and SportsSignUp. I imagine most select teams in sports today utilize some sort of digital team-management system.

Our U12 era also marked the beginning (and revealed the false importance) of parental monitoring of the team's state and national rankings (see Appendix I). Youth soccer teams become ranked on GotSoccer.com beginning at the U11 age group—something I think, frankly, is ridiculous. Most youth sports rank both teams and players (four-star recruits and such) regionally and nationally via Rivals.com, 247sports.com, Baseballyouth.com, Nyaabasketball.org, Usclublax.com, and many more. I discovered rankings for teams with kids as young as five for baseball and eight for basketball, something even crazier than what occurs in soccer.

Once Evan got to U11, rankings determined the level of tournament and league play to which his team was assigned to compete. GotSoccer's rankings cross-compare tournament and league results and weigh the results according to the strength of opponents. GotSoccer then utilizes mathematical algorithms to calculate and generate a team's "assessed" ranking.

The rankings are not absolute and definable in the same manner that college football's Football Bowl Subdivision (FBS) playoff rankings are also hugely debatable. Direct head-to-head comparison games often don't exist even among regional teams, let alone for teams from different states. As difficult as it is to nail down the components that achieve a particular ranking, as the years progressed, I did conclude that rankings reasonably segment teams into similar buckets of overall competitive ability. Also, the more tournaments in which a team plays, the better the rankings data reflect that team's relative competitive level.

The Severna Park Fury team started out with national rankings in the 300 to 600 range and a Maryland state ranking of about twenty-five, and it continuously moved up the rankings ladder. Fury leveled out by about U16, with national rankings typically in the 75 to 150 range and Maryland state rankings between five and ten.

In some respects, Fury was rankings-challenged because the team's coaches, to their credit, always entered the team in the toughest possible league and tournament brackets. This fostered player development, but it didn't generate easy wins, championships, and advantageous ranking points [==].

By example, another local Maryland team, Pachuca, was typically highly ranked in the fifteen to fifty range nationally, but it somewhat gamed the ranking system. Pachuca played in more tournaments than Fury, and it also often participated in weaker and less challenging brackets. As a result, Pachuca was regularly a champion, which adds to ranking points. Fury and Pachuca split their head-to-head games over the final few years, but Pachuca was always much higher ranked. In effect, Pachuca had sandbagged the ranking system in a manner similar to the way golfers or tennis players manage their handicaps.

Pachuca's gaming of the ranking system was nothing compared to a Northern New Jersey team (STA-MUSC 2000s), which rostered enough good regional players to make up two teams within one. With such generous participation, the team juggled player and guest rosters, enabling participation in multiple tournaments on some weekends and doubling its opportunity for wins and ranking points. At one point, this team was ranked No. 1 in the country by a fair margin of ranking points. While this team's management of the ranking system was well known, it should also be noted that it was good enough to win the Disney Showcase, a top national tournament.

Double Play

In case this new Fury team did not work out, Evan double-carded to play on the Crofton Cosmos in the BBSL league. Cosmos needed extra players for its BBSL spring season to cover for baseball players missing in action, just as Fury did. Fury games were on Saturdays and Cosmos games on Sundays, which allowed Evan to satisfy his endless need for more soccer. Cosmos was ably led by Coach Mike M, who fostered an inclusive environment. This positivity, plus a lack of pressure concerning playing time or tryouts, led to an enjoyable season of playing extra soccer just for the fun of it. Cosmos also won its league at 8–1, which resulted in an awesome dual-win spring season for Evan.

In this spring season, Fury was among just five undefeated and untied teams out of the 400 NCSL teams. NCSL follows the European approach of sorting teams according to performance, promoting the top teams up a division and relegating the bottom teams down a division. Fury moved up to NCSL's Division 4 in the fall of 2012.

After two years of bouncing between teams and getting the runaround from several coaches, Evan seemed to have landed a good fit with his teammates and coaches, and he was back to an appropriate level travel team. But playing time, rankings, and tough tryouts were new challenges thrown into the mix, and critically important tryouts were looming if Evan was to remain rostered on Fury for the upcoming fall season.

Chapter 5

How Can the U14 Opponents Drive Themselves Home?

Soccer, like many youth sports, requires teams to have their rostered players registered or "carded" to ensure players are of the appropriate age to participate in U-whatever. The "carding police" (i.e., referees) then check each player before the game to ensure that person has the appropriate age card and is officially rostered on the team.

Red Cards to the Rescue

To get a player carded or registered on a team, the team manager must submit a player's birth certificate, picture, and whatever fees are required to a designated youth organization. For soccer, a few of those organizations include U.S. Youth Soccer, the various state soccer associations (Maryland State Youth Soccer Association in our case), the U.S. Club, American Youth Soccer Organization (AYSO), and Soccer Association for Youth (SAY). Each carding organization has its own set of rules defining how many rostered players are allowed on a team, the number of teams on which each player can be rostered, the number of guest players allowed for tournaments, restrictions on moving players from team to team, and, of course, the birthdate limits of each U-whatever age group.

For the most part, I never liked the hoopla surrounding carding. Carding seemed to be another arcane administrative and bureaucratic mess that largely creates barriers to playing [==]. And, of course, where there is a rule, enterprising adults will attempt to game the system; several Little League World Series age and residency scandals quickly come to mind. Frankly, no kid ever cares about carding rules. They simply want to play the game.

Evan was lucky in his early years of double-carding, as his two teams and leagues utilized two different carding organizations. Somewhere about U13, though, navigating the carding requirements became more complicated, because most teams and leagues used the U.S. Youth Soccer cards. Evan frequently played as a guest in tournaments, as well as on the Maryland State Olympic Development Program (ODP) team, and while we were always able to work around carding requirements, on the surface, these bureaucracies mostly seemed a hurdle to playing the sport.

That was, until one U13 tournament game. In this particular game, Evan's team was stomped by something like five or six goals to zero. The opponents averaged about half a head taller, and several players had beards, a sharp contrast to our prepubescent twelve- and thirteen-year-olds. For the first time ever, carding came to the rescue. This team of near adults had all three of their tournament games forfeited due to unspecified carding violations.

Crying Foul

Evan's private high school had a couple of freshman players who had come from overseas countries. These players had passports, but apparently no official birth certificate. When the high school coach started up an associated travel team, these international players could not obtain official player cards.

One of these players had well-developed facial hair and full-on man legs at age fourteen. He participated in any travel-team game where the carding police failed to engage rigorous enforcement (a couple of games during winter blizzards, for instance). *Perhaps carding does have its place*, I began to think.

Over ten years of carding fuss, these are the only two incidents in which I personally know of players who may have blown out a few extra birthday candles. Having said that, when playing in the U12-U14 age brackets, Evan's team encountered several players who seemed to stand out as being truly beyond the intended age bracket. A few times, the opponents were well-developed boys, bearded or mustached boys, or car key-twirling boys. In each instance, player cards were checked and absolutely were in order—exactly like my extra "special" college-era driver's license indicating I was of legal drinking age.

In contrast to cheating with older players, I am aware of one coach who pushed the carding rules in the *opposite* direction, his intentions to provide younger players additional playing opportunities. He seemed to have a delightful disregard for the organizational bureaucracies. On a couple of occasions, this coach recruited younger brothers and cousins of team members when the team was shorthanded at tournaments. These younger players would just "become" an absent team member—a Billy Smith would become a Tommy Jones for the day.

In one memorable instance of carding nonsense, the ethnic appearance of a rogue guest player was obviously completely different than that pictured on the player's card. Likewise, I'd heard of an "emergency basis" card in which an apparent forgery was laminated and looked like the real deal. These transgressions involved younger guest players at U18-U19 tournaments, and no one seemed to care. In contrast, cards seemed to be more rigorously checked at the U11-U14 age level, where physical growth differentials across the players can be significant.

Evan and I encountered two other inadvertent age-related surprises during this time. Once at U13, supplemental Coach Mike B arranged a scrimmage against his "high-school freshmen" and "perhaps a few sophomore junior varsity players." The coach's high schoolers won handily, 5–1, as they were bigger, stronger, and faster, although not necessarily more skilled than the U13 travel-team players. The coach's deception was further revealed when the "JV" players all drove themselves home.

False Start

Fourteen-year-old Evan participated in summer tryouts along with as many as forty other freshmen to see who would be selected to DeMatha High School's extremely competitive program. I left work early to catch the end of the first tryout session, anxious about how his abilities would slot in.

When I arrived at the tryouts, Evan was parked on the sidelines, not playing, among three fields of players. He wasn't even being given a shot by the coaches. When finally subbed in, he played okay, but he probably wasn't in the top half of the twenty-two players present. I quickly surmised that if Evan wasn't among the freshmen top half, he would rarely, if ever, play.

How could our assessment of the high school playing level have been so wrong? I was distraught. In a flash, Evan's high school sports journey seemed to have vanished in the fifteen minutes I'd watched these freshman tryouts.

I was getting ready to console him and practicing my elevator speech to conjure up some sort of rationalization that high school athletics would somehow work out for him—that he could be coming off the bench by senior year.

Then I saw a couple of players jumping into cars and driving off. *Wow,* I thought, *these private school freshmen are far more mature than Evan and his friends.* Evan then jumped into the car with a big smile, saying, "Dad, did you see I was one of three freshmen called up to practice with the *varsity starters*?" WHEW!

Foul Play

While age and residency issues are the most common forms of cheating in youth sports, money, drugs (steroids), team switching, lack of inclusiveness, and gender issues also occur. I know of one coach who allegedly took in more money than he spent on his team's behalf. A far more common money issue revolves around teams and players forced to participate (pay) in one organizer's activity—training, camp, tournament, hotel, uniform—in order to sustain play on that organizer's roster. These pay-to-play mandates occur frequently.

Fortunately, we didn't encounter truly problematic issues of adults gaming the system, but there are many reported examples which is something all sports parents should keep in mind. We all want our kids participating on a level playing field, both literally and figuratively. When someone games the system to the point of fraud, illegally pays for roster placement or playing time, or goes to the length of securing steroids for kids, the integrity and joy of the game is stripped for everyone.

Chapter 6

The Stakes Are Bigger When It's a Teen Game (U12-U13)

When it comes to sports tryouts, nothing is more subjective than a coach's perception of an athlete's ability based on a few minutes of observation. Still, tryouts are critically important in the early teen years, when the physical development stages are most varied, and serious travel teams begin to establish the future hierarchy of play.

The Fast and Tall Bias

In baseball, coaches can consider a multitude of statistics, including batting average, on-base percentages, strikeouts, and walks. In basketball, points, shooting percentages, assists, and steals can all be tallied and analyzed. Football has passes completed, running yards, passes caught, tackles, and touchdowns. Swimming, track, and cross-country time results are measurable and definitive.

> "From a player's standpoint, they are always in a tryout."
> —Sasho Cirovski, Maryland men's soccer coach and three-time national champion

In contrast, soccer has few statistics for field players. Goals and assists are so limited that the numbers are not statistically significant. Except at the pro level, no one tracks any meaningful soccer statistics such as passes completed, tackles made, passing percentages, or distances covered. That means soccer evaluations are among the most subjective of any sport's performance evaluation [==]. Yet tryouts, combines, and rankings remain the never-ending reality of youth journeys in all sports.

Physical size and speed are two aspects coaches clearly favor, in part because they are measurable, unlike the myriad nuanced soccer skills such as footwork, moving without the ball, positioning, and field vision. Further, between ages eleven and fourteen, the physical growth differential—particularly among boys—is at its greatest. Many soccer coaches simply recruit the biggest and fastest athletes in this age range, as these aspects are simple to evaluate and a potentially easy path to winning games. While youth football also has size (weight) ranges, the weight spread within a bracket is nearly 100 percent. Wrestling may be one of the few youth sports that truly fosters narrow physical-size bands.

In addition, even those athletically gifted and chosen players may be negatively impacted by not having to focus much on their skills development. For some teams, the winning strategy is to kick the ball to the big, fast kid who then outruns the smaller kids to score. Watch a high school video of LeBron James or Shaquille O'Neal, and the concept becomes obvious.

This focus on size and athleticism has been a frequent criticism of the U.S. Men's National Soccer Team selections. Most pundits agree that the U.S. athletic focus is misguided and a potential long-term detriment to its national soccer team performance. After all, Lionel Messi, David Silva, Eden Hazard, and Sergio Aguero are no taller than 5'8." Size bias is common in other sports with comments about the relative shortness of players like Muggsy Bogues and Isiah Thomas in basketball, Julian Edelman in football, and Marta Vieira da Silva in soccer.

During this early teen period, some teams rely exclusively on their unstoppable giant for nearly all scoring and success. Over the years, Evan's coaches deployed a simple solution to counteract these oversized scoring machines: Mark them with holding midfielder Evan in an assigned man-to-man coverage. This strategy is equivalent to a defensive "box and one" tactic utilized in basketball to stop a superstar, double-team blocking an extraordinary volleyball killer, pitching around a superb hitter, or assigning a linebacker to shadow a superstar running back.

Pesky, relentless, and diminutive Evan was assigned this unique defensive task perhaps a half-dozen times. The approach completely disrupted the opposing team's solitary offensive strategy and frustrated the giant who was effectively prevented from ever getting on the ball. Sometimes the marginalized giant became so aggravated that he constantly fouled and picked up a yellow card. I can happily report that these tall, designated scorers never put the ball in the net when this defensive tactic was deployed, and Evan's team won all these games.

The subjective tryout process is so endemic in youth sports that some organizers utilize independent assessors to try to solve the problems that come with it. For example, Olympic Development Program (ODP) tryouts for the Maryland state team, in which up to several hundred players compete for a place on the roster, utilize independent assessors. Each player is provided a numbered T-shirt in one of two colors, and the assessors then assign skill-set rankings to the players trying out. A few players make the cut, and a few players will be on the cusp and need further evaluation. Most will not be selected.

The ODP tryouts were some of the fairest selection processes I observed, though it must be said that some players—even with the relative anonymity of randomly numbered T-shirts—are well known to some assessors, so no process is perfectly unbiased. Also, politics are certainly an important selection factor of most tryouts as many coaches are certain to select the athletes who are buddies with their own kids.

Several companies have recently developed digital tryout and ranking tools to try to systematize the selection process. While none of these platforms were utilized during Evan's journey (they mostly didn't exist), they are becoming ever more popular. Myteamgenius.com and Skillshark.com are two examples, and these platforms link directly to some of the rostering systems. Both tryout platforms handle most of the primary team sports (football, basketball, baseball, softball, soccer, lacrosse, cheer, field hockey, volleyball, and ice hockey), and of course, recommend independent assessors.

In another attempt to circumvent unwarranted size or athleticism bias, U.S. Soccer announced a new program in April 2018 called "bio-banding," which purports to group youth athletes based on their apparent biological age rather than chronological age. While this program has good intentions, I can foresee coaches putting together teams made up exclusively of bio-banded older athletes who are all assessed to be physically much younger than their chronological age. I also suspect "bio-banding police" will have to be established to enforce bio-banding age assessments. When there is a rule in youth sports, there's little doubt that some enterprising adult will attempt to game it.

Roughing It

The early teen years are when youth sports start to become very physical and, in many cases, full-on contact sports. Inadvertent hostile elbows, knees, and kicks become the new norm. While this kind of physicality is an obvious component to football, rugby, and ice hockey, other sports get rougher, too. Basketball has its box-outs, soccer hard slide tackles, baseball takeout slides and pitching brushbacks, wrestling takedown body slams, field hockey stick trips, and, my personal favorite, lacrosse stick checking. Aggressive travel sports, in some cases, leave more "gentle" kids behind.

Any doubts about the rough physical nature of soccer are put to rest by observing the bruises, cuts, black eyes, and other knocks the kids received while playing. In addition to legal hits, players are subjected to purposeful but illegal kicks, cleatings, elbows, stompings, and even punches. Central midfield, by its nature, has higher player density and, therefore, the most collisions. Midfielders also take additional risks with overtly aggressive play since the negative consequences of a conceded foul are minimal and the positive benefits of a potential takeaway are high.

Sometimes, referees allow games to get out of hand, and other times, players take advantage when a referee is looking in the other direction. On top of smack talk, action sports played by young teens have plenty of physical smacking. Soccer players and parents will be familiar with the term "broken ankles." This refers to an opponent who is duped or tricked ("juked") by clever play, though it is the trickster player who's most often the one getting their ankles kicked or cleated, not their duped opponent.

The central positions where Evan played tended to have the most ball possession. This led to midfielders like him incurring the most fouls over the years as opponents poked out their foot or stepped on the midfielders to defend. Even in the pros, players with strong foot skills get fouled the most. For example, the talented

Eden Hazard was among the most fouled players in the English Premier League (85 times in the 2016–17 season), due to his quick feet and changes of direction.

In our later travel-team years, fewer inadvertent fouls occurred, as the opponents became more skilled defensively. At the same time, intentional fouls increased aplenty as the players got better in their acting while making a "legitimate" attempt on the ball. Evan, for instance, increasingly made sure he was awarded the foul call by crashing down or even yelping when aggressively fouled. The embellished, flopping, and Oscar-worthy performances were left to the strikers.

Evan had a particularly rough tryout ahead of him in the spring of 2012 if he wanted to retain a roster spot on the Fury travel team for the fall of that year. The coaches were not yet sold on him due to his lack of pace, and Evan spent plenty of time on the bench whenever the whole roster showed up. His main attributes were work rate, foot skills, tenacity, and strong commitment to his team, as he never missed games or practices. In comparison, most Fury players were fast and scrawny but with perhaps somewhat weaker foot skills.

Evan did get invited to remain with the team, most likely due to the switch to eleven-player games, which required a roster expansion from fourteen to eighteen players. This switch to the larger required roster and directionally higher levels of play also resulted in a constant implementation of "roster roulette" where, over the next seven years, at least thirty-three players would come and go (see Appendix I). One particular referee may have also marginally helped Evan's chances of surviving the trying tryouts.

Referee Flu and "Volunteers"

Does any athlete, coach, or parent really like referees or umpires?

Referees are subjected to such abuse that about half quit after their first year, just 20 percent survive five years. As a consequence, many youth sports suffer a perpetual referee shortage. "Referee flu" is so rampant that the NCSL required each team to supply one linesman or assistant referee (not a center referee) for games at the U12 and U13 levels.

Where does a team find a mandatory assistant referee (AR)? From the parental ranks, of course, with yours truly being one of the two parents conscripted to don the yellow and black striped jersey. This is no different than any other youth sport that requires parents to work the locker room, concession stand, sign-up table, ticket window, or penalty box; or be a pop-up tent provider, team manager, or game photographer or videographer. In other words, parents regularly become an integral part of the youth team infrastructure.

With the AR role, the conflict of interest is obvious, yet this "voluntary" role has many underlying nuances. To NCSL's credit, we had to become officially certified referees. The final remnants of my soccer naïveté disappeared within the 140-page *Laws of the Game* rule book and fully understanding its application. Still, there are some fundamental challenges.

First, on about one out of perhaps twenty plays, the referee has no clue as to which player last touched the ball before it went out of play. Don't believe otherwise.

Second, when it comes to offside calls, the AR must observe when the ball is kicked and simultaneously look across the defensive line to see if the offensive player is in an offside position. This is an oxymoron. While the eyes of a lizard can focus on two distinct places simultaneously, forward-facing human eyes cannot. There is an underlying fraction of a second between glances. Watch any English Premier League game to confirm that even professionals get these offside calls wrong on occasion.

As parental ARs, the most important challenge we faced was gaining the trust and confidence of the impartial central referee.

The best way to gain that trust was to lean toward giving the benefit of doubt for any early game close calls to the opposing team. Naturally, we also incurred the ire of some parents with this attitude, but, thankfully, the players seemed largely indifferent.

In a couple of cases, the opponent's parental AR would make consistently and overtly biased calls in favor of his kid's team. (Note: the non-gender-neutral "his" is used correctly here, as very few of the ARs were women and none of the women we did work with were blatantly biased.) The center referee always gracefully handled these situations of biased AR calls by either ignoring or offsetting them. In the end, parents sometimes came up to me after the games and acknowledged we had called a good game, despite the occasional frustration with a call. Besides, I never once had a parent ask me to trade places and wear the yellow and black striped shirt.

Fortunately, most refs seemed impartial and did a decent job, though I would have liked to red card those few who invoked the frustration of both teams' parents. Also, I do believe that games for which we traveled some distance had a higher potential for biased calls, as the locally sourced refs may have an underlying relationship with the home team. Refereeing on the whole, though, seemed to improve as the teams got older—or perhaps I just mellowed in my assessments. The one thing I did whenever I crossed postgame paths with any ref who called a solid game is to offer a simple "Great game, ref," which always brought a smile. Positive acknowledgment was a habit I embraced from sailboat racing, where we always thanked the volunteer race managers.

Evan continued to play on the Severna Park Fury team for the 2012 fall season regardless whether my referee volunteering had any potential influence. Fury finished third in Division 4 of NCSL with a respectable 5–2–2 record. Due to his positive Crofton Cosmos experience during the spring, he also remained double-carded on the Crofton Cannons during this fall season, where he played center back.

The Cannons played in BBSL, where the team was 6–0 in the games in which Evan participated and was champion. This team provided a fantastic supplemental experience to Evan's play with Fury, thanks to an excellent team demeanor and the highly capable Coach Andrew. The Fall 2012 seasons were especially positive for Evan as Fury moved up to Division 3 of NCSL, and the Cannons moved up to Division 1 of BBSL for the spring 2013 season.

Meanwhile, Fury also won a Virginia Beach tournament about four hours away. The always tough assistant coach even provided a couple of direct compliments, among Evan's first ever from Fury management, saying, "Evan, that was your best game ever," and "You were fast running down that striker." Did Evan hear this correctly? This was honestly the first and one of the few times the word "fast" and "Evan" were used in the same sentence.

In the spring of 2013, Fury had a uniquely tough season, finishing with a 2–6–1 record in Division 3 of NCSL. Evan, among a few other players, was not in particular favor with the coaches. Fury conceded 27 goals, but the regularly benched Evan was on the field for just six of those opponent goals, and one lone goal came through his position. Still, the coaches didn't seem to notice his defensive effectiveness objectively, nor care about the ultra-low utilization of him and several of his teammates.

The coaching mood was somber with an overriding vibe that changes were needed to turn around the team's results. Most teams inevitably end up with some losing seasons, and while no one likes to be in that position, it does help athletes build character—to a point. A few teams do end up as perpetual losers for whatever reason, and I can only imagine that those situations can seem to be a long-term downward spiral for both coaches and players. Just think of the Detroit Lions, Cleveland Browns, or Chicago Cubs fans. (The Cubs did turn around their 100-plus year dearth of success in 2016). Evan, fortunately, experienced only a couple of tough seasons and as well, typically had some alternative positive soccer activities among his repertoire.

During this period, Evan continued to supplement his play by double-carding with Cannons, who were 6-2 overall and again season champs. He particularly enjoyed his experience with Cannons, as the playing environment was hugely positive and fun. In contrast, Fury scheduling conflicts and coaching intensity were both growing with expanded league and tournament commitments.

Indeed, it was by far Fury's worst season, with the toughest tryouts to date still looming for all players. The challenge of impending assessments that have an incessant focus on size, speed, and strength (and with perhaps a small dash of politics thrown in) versus actual skills is a never-ending constant in youth sports from peewees all the way through to the professional ranks [==]. Young athletes have no control over their physical stature, and while a few kids have natural athleticism, that wasn't the case for Evan and most of his peers.

> "Since the combine started, NFL teams have come to overvalue the things that can be measured (height, strength, speed) and undervalue the sort of intangibles (intelligence, creativity, will) that make for winning teams." —Rich Cohen, sportswriter

In this twelve- to thirteen-years age era, the youth game almost instantly transitions into a "big kids" game. Maybe half the kids' growth spurts had started to kick in. Likewise, the intensity and expectations of travel sports were growing exponentially. Taken together, the stakes in youth sports appeared to loom larger and larger. This age period seemingly marked the point of no return when it comes to most kids committing to one sport—assuming they remained selected.

Chapter 7

Sports Means More

While many families have spare shoes, dog toys, and unread magazines lying around their family room floors, ours always had an assortment of soccer balls distributed around the house. Soccer balls are not a décor item, of course, but rather an object that must be readily available for use. Moms, tables, and the pet dog should be regularly nutmegged (ball passed between their legs), shouldn't they? Who knows when the juggling urge might suddenly be required to help relieve teen angst? Karen has been a great sport about this, but she has stored many breakable objects away for safekeeping over the last ten years.

Anywhere There's a Ball

I have seen similar sports décor in the homes of basketball, football, baseball, softball, volleyball, and lacrosse devotees. Many parents wisely resort to wiffle balls, nerf balls, or soft plastic pucks to limit the damage wrought by the inevitable indoor play.

Likewise, the mudroom or entranceway of so many sports-focused homes waft that special locker room scent.

While I did hear the occasional crash, bang, or loud exclamation of “Oops!” (or other unpublishable four-letter word), fortunately, our home and belongings never incurred any major damage, unlike the two windows I took out with a baseball as a kid. At the same time, I have to admit that the occasional bouts of hall soccer against me definitely got out of hand—but a few dirty ball imprints on the walls are a minor decorating inconvenience for the benefit of wall bounce passes which are a key strategy.

Hall soccer is for wimps compared to elevator soccer (think futsal on steroids). Evan and I played elevator soccer in many hotels where we stayed for travel games, and surprisingly, we never once got reprimanded. Our favorites were towered hotels where each closed-door session could last a minute or more. We did occasionally receive stunned looks on guests’ faces when the elevator doors opened on us with a ball still in play.

I’ve also seen hockey teams playing hall knee hockey. Apparently, hotel hallways just seem to attract spontaneous combustion of wiffle ball games, dribbling contests, volleyball bump-pass challenges, LAX passing drills, softball baserunning pickle, and field hockey shooting challenges. The issue is so widespread that some hotels hosting teams now make the kids sign promises during registration not to engage in these indoor sports activities.

Road Games

As I said in an earlier chapter, Evan started extra training beginning at age eight. Since then, he has continuously undertaken a variety of supplemental skills building or physical training regimens. His team’s two scheduled practices a week never seemed enough for him, nor did the six years he was either double-carded (two teams) or playing on Maryland’s state ODP team. In some double-carding seasons, he would practice Mondays and Wednesdays with one team and then Tuesdays and Thursdays with the other, and he'd play a Saturday game with one team and a Sunday game with the other. (For most of our double-carding seasons, the two teams, fortunately, did not play their games on the same weekend day.) We recognized that this single-sport focus goes against the grain of well-roundedness recommended by nearly all sports doctors and coaches, but Evan always wanted more soccer.

Occasionally, the two teams did have games on the same day, and we had to commute from a morning southern Virginia game to an afternoon northern Maryland game, or vice versa. Directly conflicting games were rare, but in a few cases, I had the pedal to the metal to make the second game while Evan rehydrated and adeptly changed uniforms in the car. While rushing to make two games was challenging, we had only a couple of minor logistical boo-boos along the way. Once or twice we arrived at a field and Evan said, "Hey, Dad, where are my teammates?" Likewise, GPS and iPhone directions are great except when they guide us to the wrong destination: "Dad, there are no soccer fields at the end of this cul-de-sac." The huge new sportplexes can also be daunting—*Where the heck is field 137 anyway?* Through all of these foibles, somehow, we never missed a game.

Follow Through

Outside of team practice and games, Evan and I played extra soccer together for about six years, beginning with our backyard practices when he was age eight. I was no different in supporting my kid's sports interests than the fathers of such well-known and diverse superstars as Joe Montana, Kobe Bryant, Chris Evert, Ken Griffey Jr., Mark Howe, Kyle Petty, Serena Williams, Dale Berra, Brett Hull, and Cal Ripken.

Evan and I worked on passing drills, Dribbling Around Cones 101, Shooting Practice 202, Ball Control 303, and lots of making runs across the yard to score against each other. These runs were soccer's equivalent of playing "H-O-R-S-E" in basketball, with the first getting to ten or fifteen goals declared the winner.

By age ten, Evan had outgrown our confined yard. His elementary and middle school was about a mile from our house and had a small turf field that was sparingly utilized during non-school hours. Evan and I commandeered this field as our own for the next four years, practicing there for a couple of hours most weekends and holidays. We often stopped by the field on the way home from games or practices for "more."

In this developmental period, I noticed most young players mainly employed their dominant foot and had limited control of the ball with their weak foot. Most kids ran around the ball to kick it only with their dominant foot. With that knowledge, I concentrated on passing balls to Evan's weaker left foot, perhaps favoring the left foot by as much as 80 percent of all the balls passed to him over several years. By constantly forcing balls onto his left foot, Evan's non-dominant foot control and strength greatly improved, and he became much closer to being ambidextrous than most players. Even though he played mostly central positions, a few coaches moved him to the left side because of his solid left-foot skills (left backs and wingers benefit from control as they work to keep the ball inbounds along the left-side touchline.)

We developed more of our own drills from there. For example, at each practice I laid out cones across the length of the turf field, and Evan made multiple dribbling runs to try to get another "record" time. My stopwatch was always at the ready. When we started, his quickest cone runs were in the mid-twenty seconds. Four years later, he was completing the drill in well under ten seconds.

In other drills, we maintained mental records of consecutive penalty shots, juggling, right-foot and left-foot chip backs to me, alternating-foot chip backs, passes between cones from increasing distances, winners of "soccer tennis," and any other measurable shorthanded drill we could invent. Occasionally, a buddy would join us, which opened up the possibilities for two-against-one drills and, much to my lament, playing keep-away from Dad.

Perhaps the most important aspect of these training sessions was that a 70- to 110-pound kid was practicing against a 175-pound adult. His years of constant practice against a much larger opponent made him fearless playing against bigger kids in games. What do twenty pounds or a few inches matter when a kid regularly practices against someone twice their size? A couple of times, I did inadvertently deck him out due to my one hundred-pound mass advantage. He somehow always picked himself up off the turf and then determinedly worked to crush me even more.

These supplemental practices ended abruptly when Evan turned fourteen due to the confluence of two events.

> "The difference for kids at this level is the amount of repetition that they get ... The more of this your kids can get, the better ... This is the one constant I have found with players that reached the major leagues ... someone spent time with them away from the field." —Mike Matheny, MLB manager, former player, and youth advocate

First was an issue of physical speed. Until he turned thirteen, I had the speed advantage, and through that first teen year our speeds were about even. Now, at fourteen, he'd become too fast for me to defensively cover—he could just buzz right by me.

High school was the other issue, as practicing with Dad was no longer "cool." He'd sometimes take part in a few shooting practices where I played keeper and shagged balls. I even bought him two mannequin dummies to enable pressured shooting practice with fixed defenders, but the dummies quickly became garage-bound dust collectors. To me it was clear that our practicing days were over, as the best I could muster was Youth Soccer 202, while Evan had moved on to graduate school.

Sports Means More

Playing on two teams and supplemental practices with a parent would have quelled most kids' appetite for their sport, but not Evan's. After all these years, he still wanted more sports time, and that means I was always searching to find that time. In 2011, I found it with "Soccer Means More."

Coach Nate started Soccer Means More as a supplemental training program for youth players serious about the game. Coach Nate played at the D1 level and is a masterful teacher, able to pass on specific skill sets to individual players unlike any other coach encountered along the journey.

One thing Coach Nate promoted was the importance of explosive speed, strength, and conditioning. Soccer Means More training sessions always included on-the-ball work (ball skills) and an equally important off-the-ball segment (physical training) with sidekick Coach Ryan B. It was through Coach Nate that the importance of physical training was embedded into Evan's psyche, and it's something that's still with him today. He was also one of few coaches who positively addressed the psychological side to each individual's approach to sports.

Evan lucked out during his second year (2012–13) of Soccer Means More training. Strictly on the age basis of twelve to thirteen, he was slotted to practice with the younger group but was by far the strongest player among it. Coach Nate moved him up to play with the fourteen to seventeen age group of perhaps twelve players, several of whom became D1 college athletes.

This year of supplemental training with older players significantly accelerated Evan's competence on the ball and his speed of play. He had no choice. It was either get the ball off his feet on his own or a big, fast, strong player would happily remove it for him. Practices were fast, faster still for a skilled but challenged thirteen-year-old. Fortunately, the older players could not complain, as Evan was better than half of the older players, though clearly no match for the best players.

Supplements

I never found another Coach Nate who focused so well on each individual player's assessment and development [==]. As a result, we had to adjust Evan's supplemental training approaches over his last four years of youth sports. We ramped up camp attendance from ages fourteen through seventeen; Evan attended twenty-seven college camps, an average of almost seven per year. A few camps ended up not being worth it because the level of play tended to revert to the lowest common denominator of attending players, but at least half the camps provided a challenging and worthwhile training environment.

In addition to regular camp attendance, Evan began to do training runs outside of team practices, including five-mile distance runs and tough "beep-test" (back and forth shuttle) sprint training. For strength training, we bought benches and weights plus a membership to Gold's Gym. Both were smart moves, especially during the high school offseason where Evan made gains in strength and developed six-pack abs that would do justice to any exercise infomercial.

At one point, he tried out a training specialist with a soccer background, but Evan felt doing extra training runs himself was just as effective. Any dedicated athlete can train well on their own by using some old-school cones and a stopwatch. For those wishing for something "shinier" in their training, a myriad of technologies is now in use. These include GPS, video, wearables, tracking, radar, laser, sensors, data analysis, performance metrics, digital apps, and others that measure and evaluate speed, strength, agility, quickness, vision, response time, positioning, biomechanics, effect on the surface or field or ball or puck, and other sports-related performance measures. These are often combined with big-data analytics to measure performance progress.

These training technologies and their companies are growing rapidly. Some of today's more prominent companies include Parisi Speed School, Velocity Sports Performance, EXOS, Velopro Sports, and Vizual Edge, among many others. To show the growing scale of sports technology, even mega-companies Microsoft and SAP are directly involved in data analytics. In addition, many of these companies provide sport-specific training and metrics; Catapult Sports, Performa Sports, Soccer Genius, and iSoccerPath have dedicated soccer applications. These technology trends arrived too late for Evan and his teammates, but technology-based training is poised to be more pervasive in the future. Current thinking is that the pandemic of 2020 likely accelerated the utilization of individualized and segregated training methodologies like these.

Leaving no supplemental training stone unturned, Evan sought out any opportunity for extra soccer touches that he could find. A nearby indoor sports facility operated drop-in futsal sessions on weekend nights from ten until midnight for adults. Futsal is a high-speed, five-versus-five soccer-styled game played on a hardcourt surface. Futsal requires extremely fast footwork and thinking; players have almost no time and space on the pocket-sized pitch, so the sport is one of reflex and reaction, a short-sided soccer on steroids.

While the sessions had no enforced age requirement, youths did not participate until they could physically compete with adults. For Evan, that began at age fifteen. These futsal sessions promoted fun and inventive free play. While playing time was rotated fairly, winners stayed on the court. A few times, some regulars and Evan stacked their teams' lineups, resulting in almost two hours of nonstop and exhaustive play because they hardly lost. There were a lot of smiles at the end of these fun evenings. The only real challenges with these late-night sessions were that I had to forego adult beverages and drive my teen there and back at awful hours on weekend nights.

Unlike many kids, Evan undertook supplemental training throughout his youth-sports journey—he never wavered. This training also taught him the importance of always hustling, not just in games and particularly in practices. His constant training transformed a thick, slow, and somewhat unathletic rec league player into a solid, better-accomplished athlete. When you're not a natural athlete, that's what it takes to sustain performance.

To this day, soccer balls remain on standby throughout our house.

Chapter 8

Tournacations, 180,000 Miles, and Seven Inches That Made a Difference (U13-U14)

Like hockey, tennis, and basketball, soccer is a fluid game. This fluidity occurs across the whole pitch, not only with dribbling and passing but also moving without the ball, taking and filling in open space, defensively man-marking, and working give-and-gos. Soccer's incessant fluid movements are what truly makes it the beautiful game, I eventually discovered. But all that fluidity isn't confined to the playing fields. Elite travel sports also mandate embracing movement along the interstate highway system.

Tournacation

When Evan was just ten years old, his team traveled as far as ninety minutes from home for a forty-minute game. That's a five-hour process for perhaps thirty minutes of action. By age thirteen, the commutes had expanded to two-and-a-half hours for a sixty-minute game, meaning players, parents, and coaches now had to commit seven hours for perhaps forty minutes of action. Bigger, multi-game tournaments were generally two to five hours away. When players are fifteen, commutes for regional travel-league games took up to nine hours each way, the only saving grace being the infrequency of these extreme distances.

Hotels became a necessity and expense for distant games. Away league games were often paired up on Saturday and Sunday while tournaments were always comprised of three games taking place Friday through Sunday. We also learned the travel player art form of washing socks and uniforms in the hotel sink with shampoo followed by drying over the heater/AC vent, a feat made possible by the uniforms' synthetic materials that readily dried overnight.

For one extreme winter game in upstate New York, the team decided to save hotel expenses and drive up from Maryland in the morning. The boys got up early and rode six hours in a toasty car to a field that, as far as we could tell, was adjacent to the Arctic Circle. The warmups became a literal challenge to get warm at all, with Canadian winds howling through the area. The frozen tundra was more hockey rink than field. The team went through the motions and played a crappy, lethargic, eighty-minute game in the bitter cold before we wearily saddled up for the six-hour sleigh ride back.

Our stiff and tired team lost, 1–0, to the much weaker locals; the stress and time that travel takes are why home teams across all sports win more games. Commuting twelve hours for one horrible game was not a great way to spend a Saturday, but these exhausting trips were, fortunately, only an occasional part of the journey. Still, our regional travel paled in comparison to that of an academy-level soccer team that reported, during one league season, its *closest* away game was 800 miles distant.

The distances to travel-team games can sometimes be absurd.

We were lucky to live in suburban Maryland, one of the nation's hotbeds for field sports. For the most part, league commutes were limited to about ninety minutes, as the Maryland-Virginia region was home to plenty of challenging teams. In fact, many national championship teams have come from this central East Coast region. Evan's team played the number-one ranked team many times over the years.

Our region also was big in the "tournacation" of soccer by sponsoring top national showcase tournaments, including the Bethesda, Potomac, Jefferson, Columbia, and Richmond Cups. In these tournaments, opposing teams traveled into our region from as far away as Maine, Florida, and Texas [==], but Evan's Maryland team had to travel just one to three hours.

Maryland is home to two major field complexes. The Soccerplex has twenty-three fields and can boast that it's the home base of the U.S. Women's National Team. The smaller Centennial Park has nine fields. Virginia and Delaware also have large, multi-field complexes, in addition to thirty-eight fields that are temporarily installed on a sod farm in Southern New Jersey each spring, all just a couple of hours away.

While our local teams have access to some amazing field collectives, this "sportsplexing" of America has taken on a national presence. Many sportsplexes now have ten- to even twenty-plus outdoor fields, many Astroturfed to enable all-weather competition. These support the tournacation of sports including field hockey, lacrosse, football, ultimate frisbee, and, of course, soccer. Similarly, large baseball/softball sportsplexes with multiple diamonds radiating from central hubs like spokes of a wheel are now commonplace. As an example, Grand Park Sports Campus in Westfield, Indiana, features twenty-six baseball and softball diamonds. Some towns even support arrays of sportsplexes such as the four found in Kissimmee, Florida. As impressive as those facilities are, the scale of the largest, the fifty-two-field National Sports Center in Blain, Minnesota, is hard to imagine.

Court sports have seen a similar explosion of the sportsplex establishment. These indoor facilities support basketball, volleyball, cheer, and badminton competitions. The LakePoint Sports campus outside of Atlanta, Georgia, is one of the biggest, able to host twelve basketball or twenty-four volleyball games simultaneously. And, as the popularity of these facilities grows, many cities are linking area sportsplexes with access to school and collegiate facilities to further support the broad expansion of youth-sports tournament play.

Taken for a Ride

Travel sports provided an unexpected benefit to our parent and child relationship in that Evan was a captive audience during our multi-hour commutes without the distraction of TV, computers, homework, friends, girlfriends, or FIFA games. Once in the car—typically our soccer mom minivan—my child had no means of escape from me. Oh, sure, commutes were partially lost to naps and gaming, Instagram posts, and Snapchats on the dreaded mobile phone. But these long drives provided plenty of inescapable father-son chat time.

Sports commutes also helped accumulate 180,000 miles on our decidedly uncool Honda minivan over eleven years, the majority of which Karen accumulated driving to and from practices. I sometimes wonder if minivan or SUV ownership is an unwritten requirement of families involved in youth sports. Either vehicle can haul seven athletes to games, practices, and postgame ice cream outings, thanks to their three rows of seats. Of course, SUVs have more caché and would have been our kids' preferred vehicle of choice—but they weren't paying the bills.

Our family, of course, embraced the *joie de vie* that soccer had become for Evan and his teammates, with the requisite magnetic soccer ball and ODP and NCSL stickers pasted on the tailgate to affirm our total allegiance to soccer. We did not go as far as a soccer mom vanity plate, but ours was truly a youth-sports minivan complete with the hard-earned detritus of sweat-infused artificial "turf turds" smeared in the floor mats, food crumbs accumulating in every conceivable crevice, innumerable empty water bottles, always a half-empty case of full water bottles, and a vivid assortment of discarded snack wrappers. Our minivan, at times, pulsed as if it were a moving biohazard experiment.

What did Evan and I talk about on these trips? Soccer, school, playing time, the hard work needed to achieve objectives, soccer, playing time, girls, homework, buddies, English Premier League, drugs and alcohol, soccer, playing time, doing well in school, working out, the universe, cars, soccer, playing time, girls, life, his commitment to objectives, soccer, playing time, and even the occasional existential subject. Did I mention soccer and playing time?

Nearly all sports psychology pundits advise parents against talking with their kids about the game and performance on the ride home. What a bunch of bull. No passionate teen athlete is going to sit quietly in a car for three hours on the way home and *not* discuss the coaches' utilization of players, personal performance, teammate performance, referee performance, idiotic screaming parents, jerk opponents and, of course, playing time. While I tried never to "car coach," it was only natural to chat about the game.

To keep these conversations positive, I always noted and commended Evan's several best plays. But, in contradiction to the pundits' advice, the topic of his shortcomings was never avoided, not the least because Evan himself brought them up. He was always tough on himself, even if he gave the ball away just a couple of times and the turnovers failed to amount to anything. Soccer's perpetually low scores highlight that it is a sport of constant failure, but Evan took his performance seriously and hated when he messed up even a little. In fact, he would be almost angry when he felt he'd delivered a subpar performance, so I am thankful he balanced that harsh self-criticism by being fairly good at letting go of the tough game losses, unlike some teammates.

Miles and Inches

After the Spring 2013 season, tryouts loomed to remain rostered with the Fury team for the still frequently benched Evan. While selection was uncertain, he had one small résumé credit toward potential retention: Evan had been selected to play for Maryland's state ODP team, the lone Fury field player—two goalkeepers also played on ODP—with this accomplishment.

Throughout Fury's challenging 2013 spring season, Evan also practiced and played with the ODP and Cannons teams. In the final tournament, the ODP coach, surprisingly, moved the diminutive Evan to center back. He played three strong games, didn't let any opponent get past him, and was the only player who was never subbed out. The state-level selection by independent coaches may have helped save his roster spot on Fury, but his continual supplemental training was starting to translate into stronger skills and improved play on the field.

The Fury team deserved to be relegated to a lower division based on its losing record, but the coaches successfully lobbied to remain in the NCSL Division 3 for the Fall 2013 season. The coaches then revamped the player lineup, even cutting a couple of long-term regulars. With those changes, Fury improved to 7–2 and moved from second-to-last to second in Division 3. The goals conceded declined to a league-leading six, which was an enormous improvement over the twenty-seven conceded the prior season. Fury's focus on successful defense propelled it on to NCSL Division 2 for 2014.

The 2014 spring season started off slowly with a record of 0–2–2. Then, Fury magically ran off five wins in a row to achieve second place in its division at 5–2–2. Fury conceded just eight goals that equaled the best in the division. With the Fall 2014 season skipped (for the final four years of youth sports, many travel teams don't play in the fall seasons to avoid conflicting with high school schedules), Fury moved up to Division 1 in spring 2015.

By now, Evan and another player had become interchangeable in the two central midfield roles. Depending upon how rotations and substitutions worked out, sometimes the other player would end up as the holding (defensive) central midfielder position, while Evan would be assigned the attacking (offensive) central midfielder role. Both strongly preferred the other's position, and I would say their skills were better suited to their opposite assignments. The two players developed a secret pact to quietly switch into their preferred positions as soon as the natural flow of play allowed. Evan smoothly drifted back toward defense while his teammate slid forward toward offense. This secret switcheroo sequence occurred perhaps twenty times over a two-year span, and never once did the coaches comment, object, or reposition the players. Sometimes the athletes may be their own best coach.

In the Spring 2014 season, the Fury coaches added games in the Eastern Development Program (EDP) league. EDP represented a broader regional representation of teams, with those from Delaware, Pennsylvania, New Jersey, and New York participating in addition to the usual assembly of Maryland and Virginia teams. In essence, EDP was just another adult reorganization of travel-team play.

EDP helped feed Evan's ceaseless appetite for more, and this time he was able to return to playing in two leagues and two games each weekend but without the challenge of shuttling between different travel teams. Fury finished a respectable 5–2–1 in Division 2 of EDP South. Nothing like accumulating further car mileage on Interstate 95, not to mention the thirty-five dollars in tolls and more in gas for each several-hour journey to the northern hinterlands.

The miles and miles in a vehicle aside, travel sports at this level are also a game of inches—the ball or puck hitting the goalposts, offsides or first down by a nose, a fingertip save, a chest lean to break the tape, a foul ball by an inch, a ball nipping the service line or just barely rimming off the cup.

Evan's increasing success had everything to do with seven measly but critical inches. In the fourteen months up to May 2014, his genes finally kicked into overdrive and he sprouted more than seven inches. The weed averaged a half an inch per-month growth, which didn't slow down until he reached 5'7", about average for a fourteen-year-old. With that growth, short and thick Evan had vanished, it seemed, almost overnight—and, suddenly, he was among the faster players.

Chapter 9

How Adults Muck Up Youth Sports

How adults muck up youth sports, let me count the ways...

Adult muck-ups are endemic to all youth sports. I'm sure every sports parent can identify with at least some of the anecdotes that follow, none of which I made up. While some athletes benefit more than they suffer by working through these issues, the majority of kids hang up their cleats, gloves, or sticks and leave youth sports behind.

Playing Versus Winning

The first, worst, and most prevalent youth-sports issue is lack of playing time for so many kids [==]. This issue probably began with cavemen when selecting who would participate in the hunt. The issue in youth sports was openly recognized as early as 1964 when Bill Hughes started his "Everyone Plays" initiative as a central focus of his soccer program.

Unfortunately, the playing-time issue starts with peewees below age seven and remains a constant challenge throughout any athlete's journey. While normally associated with team sports, playing time even pervades individual sports such as swimming, track, cross country, tennis, golf, and sailing once kids get to high school and individual performances are agglomerated into a team score. I understand that select sports don't guarantee equal playing time, but certainly playing time at the peewee and recreation league levels should be reasonably distributed, right?

Wrong!

Everyone deep down knows the unbalanced approach to playing time is wrong for kids' development, at least at the earliest stages and in any casual (rec league) sports environment. Legions of kids quit sports because it's just a drag to sit on a bench watching other kids having fun. Too, coaches just don't know how kids are going to turn out during those early ages, so playing time for all becomes more critical both from an overall and an individual participation perspective. One of the local original B team players is now a D1, all-conference collegiate athlete, and who knew that some of the slightly overweight and slower kids would eventually make it to collegiate sports?

> "Remember this basic truth: your child will not get any better sitting on the bench and watching other kids play."
> —Rick Wolff, former baseball professional and leading youth sports advocate

Some may question why a lack of playing time at these early ages is even an issue at all. I believe the problem stems directly from the atmosphere we live in today in which adults (parents and coaches) overemphasize that little Billy or Susie must win [==]. That kind of pressure at young ages is nothing short of destructive.

Young kids should just be allowed to play the game without a focus on wins, rankings, trophies, or medals. Sports play should be focused on positive youth development rather than blue ribbons for everyone.

It's not just parents but also the coaches who get this playing time issue seriously wrong. Besides the psychological benefits, bench players with fresh legs often outperform tired starters toward the ends of halves and games. The substitutes may not score, but they do have energy to wear out the opposing team—and subs *always* play hard to try to impress.

Hockey teams play with three complete lines. Football and lacrosse regularly change lines for offense and defense. Basketball and football have time-out breaks. Soccer is the only sport where kids as young as twelve are asked to run continuously for forty-five minutes—*it's ridiculous when coaches don't substitute.*

Through the years, I observed a couple of clever soccer coaches who made wholesale substitutions of five-plus players every fifteen to twenty minutes. These teams seemed to always steamroll their opponents during the second half. I've also watched John Calipari of Kentucky and the NBA's Phil Jackson use platooning at the highest levels of basketball. If pro coaches employ this tactic, I cannot understand why so many youth coaches don't utilize fresh legs to their advantage.

Even in professional soccer, with its very limited substitution rules, how many times have we seen a coach substitute a player with fifteen minutes remaining, and that sub ends up scoring a goal? This substitute is likely not as good as the starter but has the advantage of fresh legs and energy. While I grew to understand the game of soccer, to this day, I don't get the poor utilization of solid youth players by so many coaches. This issue is a commonly reported complaint and seems endemic in many large-rostered team sports.

Without a doubt, I wanted to see my kid play regardless of the game's outcome. So, like most parents, I monitored playing time, since it wasn't doled out in fair dosages to so many kids throughout their time in sports. My sideline compatriots also wanted to see their kids get reasonable playing time: parents attended games to watch their kids play, *not* to see the team win. Unfortunately, we sports parents are complicit in fostering an environment where many youth coaches consider winning to be their primary objective. This is further reinforced by those parents whose kids are guaranteed playing time due to ability or, just as likely, some sort of favoritism.

Who am I kidding? Despite believing in a reasonable distribution of playing time, I probably am an inadvertent contributor to the winning problem as well. Otherwise, why would I have maintained records throughout the years that show Evan's teams winning 54 percent of its games and losing just 33 percent (see Appendix I).

The 2018 Winter Olympics were an excellent example of how the U.S.'s emphasis on winning might be totally wrong. Norway, with its population of five million, absolutely crushed the medal count over the countries with behemoth institutions of organized sports. In contrast to the U.S., Norway has rules against keeping scores in organized sports until age thirteen because the emphasis is on the kids developing and having fun. Interestingly, one area of U.S. Olympic success was in the snowboard events, sports in which its youth participation originates in a totally unstructured manner, akin to the neighborhood pickup games of basketball and baseball. In fact, totally autonomous activities like snowboarding, skateboarding, and BMX bike riding (think X Games) are among the fastest-growing sports in the U.S..

"Our obsession with winning is the enemy of excellence in youth sports. We have turned our attention away from developing excellence in our athletes and now only focus on immediate success." —John O'Sullivan, former soccer professional and leading youth sports advocate

Nearly all sports psychology pundits agree that the emphasis on winning during early youth stages is not ideal. To deemphasize this win-at-all-costs psychology, I often repeated this question to Evan: "If you play two million games and exclude ties, how many games will you win?" The answer is the same regardless of sport or player (LeBron, Brady, Serena, Messi, Federer, etc., excluded): If any ordinary player competes in zillions of games, the statistical odds indicate they will win half and lose half.

I witnessed a prime example of this parental focus on winning during Evan's Spring 2010 season with his Red Storm team. Red Storm was undefeated and playing the also undefeated Baltimore Bays team in the final game of the season, the winner taking the championship. The Baltimore Bays organization had produced the strongest regional soccer teams with more national championships than any other organization in the country. While respected, the Bays were also the local "evil empire" organization because its teams lost so infrequently.

Red Storm's Coach John was away for this last game, so coaching duties fell to Assistant Coach Oscar. Oscar was enthusiastic but perhaps a bit naughty—he not only scouted the Bays, but also videotaped one of their games. The Red Storm team knew the Bay's strongest player was a redheaded kid on the right side who always cut the ball back to his left foot, just like the pro's Arjen

Robben of Bayern Munich. In addition, they could plainly see that a longhaired kid on the left side cut the ball back to his right foot, as he had zero left-foot skills, and a very large player in the middle had to be covered only early in each half before he ran out of gas and became a statue.

Red Storm covered the redhead's left foot, longhair's right foot, and the big kid for the first fifteen minutes of each half. The final score was 3–1 in favor of the Red Storm, delivering yet another league championship for Evan—but did we as parents set the ideal example for youth sports?

Benched, a.k.a. Striking Out without an At-Bat

During one of Evan's periods of low playing time, I scoured books, articles, and the web for any worthwhile advice. Little is written on how to overcome this issue of inappropriate youth playing time. I found plenty of acknowledgments that the practice is fundamentally wrong, but not how to resolve it.

What guidance I did find mainly revolved around talking with the coach—which millions of players and parents do to no benefit. It's often like talking to a brick wall.

Let's be frank. Some coaches are not fully honest, and some even outright lie, to the bench-sitting kids in these discussions because coaches need them on the roster for practices, in instances of injuries, sickness, and conflicts that arise, and perhaps even to spread costs around. One alternative is for the player to move down (concede) a level of play to ensure they get playing time. A second but difficult to accomplish remedy is if the player can somehow work especially hard to ramp up their skill sets to a level comparable to or better than the starters and favorites.

This issue of playing time also has huge consequences on a kid's confidence. Over the years, I saw many bench players finally get subbed in, only to play nervously from a lack of confidence that would, of course, have been gained through regular play. They were just so afraid of making any small mistake, which for them meant a prompt one-way ticket back to the bench. Those who weren't overly nervous still knew the stakes were high and often played too cautiously and flawlessly to avoid getting immediately pulled off the field. Favored players, on the other hand, never had to worry about attempting a tough pass or taking a purely whimsical shot.

Anyone who's played sports knows it takes a few minutes to get into the game's flow and gain a feel for the opponents' level of play. Long-term bench sitters never fully or ideally develop this aptitude as they play with constant underlying fear. Internally, they know the coach doesn't have confidence in them, and that, too, perpetuates mediocre performance.

Because they lack their coach's confidence, bench sitters often feel they can never be 100 percent honest with that coach about their issues or concerns, no matter how small—a niggling minor injury, slight cold, school conflict, or preferred playing position. If a bench player advises a coach about any personal issue, that probably translates to zero minutes of play, maybe even for a couple of games. Having experienced rolled ankles, sore knees, and even the flu, Evan summarized his consistent communication approach with all coaches as, "I never once talked to a coach about any issue, as you just never, *ever* give a coach a reason not to play you." His view tells the sad reality of how many athletes feel they must manage their relationship with adult coaches. Playing time is one thing, but these less than ideal interactions with adults are also likely contributors to some kids playing with concussions and other significant injuries.

I did find one excellent web article on the playing time issue by Dr. Alan Goldberg entitled, "Hey Coach, What's Wrong with You?" It correctly indicates that the issues are not always the player's fault or due to ability and effort. We shared this article with Evan, which seemed to help his acceptance of the issue during one of the periods of low playing time.

Today, many youth-sports psychologists and coaches offer a range of mental support to help athletes deal with their internal or external issues in order to achieve peak performance levels. Evan never required any professional support—he naturally exhibited plenty of determination and grit. However, lack of confidence can become a major issue for youth athletes, and an issue that is exacerbated by coaches delivering preferential, and therefore confidence-building, treatment to their favorites.

We also regularly reminded Evan about the many kids who just fell by the wayside as his sports journey progressed. New players arrived from time to time, but many more left. Kids moved, got injured, lost interest, changed to other sports, dropped out because of grades, didn't progress in skills, or never hit their growth spurt. For Evan, his perseverance turned out to be an eventual winner. Elite youth sports are definitely a game of attrition, and sometimes the steady tortoise ends up beating the hare.

There is one more factor affected by the issue of playing time: The converse of not playing certain kids sufficiently results in overplaying the favored kids. Late in Evan's youth-sports journey, I felt he should have been subbed *out* more. So goes the world of the enduring tortoise.

Changing the Lineup, Again and Again

A structural issue in the game of soccer comes into being when the switch is made from eight-versus-eight play to eleven-versus-eleven full-field games. This switch causes absolute roster chaos as teams must increase rosters from fourteen to eighteen players. Any team losing just a couple of players immediately become unviable with only ten to twelve remaining players, and that leaves them out in the cold or they must take on much weaker players to sustain a viable roster. This tumultuous restructuring of teams and players takes a couple of years to sort out [==].

Complicating this issue, some organizations, states, leagues, and tournaments started eleven-versus-eleven play at U12, while others began this roster increase at U13 [==]. This also contributes to the roster re-sorting being unnecessarily spread over several years. Interestingly, most pundits recommend short-sided play for longer. Soccer power Spain is an example, where short-sided play continues as late as U15. As a result, short-sided games through U12 were supported by a national policy change implemented by U.S. Soccer in August 2015. While this was a change ostensibly in the right direction, it highlights the challenges of adults constantly changing the rules impacting the kids.

In reality, we adults have mucked up the transition to adult-sized constraints far too early: U12 players are not ready for full-field play [==]. They don't have the stamina for full-size fields, the leg strength to kick balls across the field, goalkeepers tall enough for a full-size, eight-foot net (the average eleven-year-old is 4'8" for boys and 4'9" for girls), or the strength to effectively make goal kicks anywhere near the halfway line.

The exploitation of shorter goalkeepers is even a common strategy utilized for a few years after the switch to full-sized goals. For one rec league U12 team, defender Evan took all the goal kicks since the keeper could not effectively kick and clear the ball upfield. (It should be noted that this weakness provided the opponents an immediate opportunity to take advantage of not being offsides due to Evan's positioning.)

Another structural age issue was that the different organizational bureaucracies utilized different age-group bracketing [==]. When Evan started soccer, most U.S. organizations utilized the school-year calendar from August 1 through July 31 to set the age brackets for youth play. In contrast, ODP, academy, national, and international organizations all utilized the calendar year from January 1 through December 31 to set age brackets.

Anyone questioning whether these four months makes a difference should read Malcolm Gladwell's *Outliers*. Gladwell outlines how the majority of professional Canadian hockey players tend to have birthdays early in the calendar year. These players were more physically advanced in their youth hockey years and benefitted from improved youth development. Simply put, during their younger years, older athletes within the same age group range have significant physical and athletic advantages that translate to favored selection and development. The scientific community even has a term for this issue: the relative age effect. Favorable early selection essentially becomes a self-fulfilling prophecy for later athletic performance.

These age ranges provided Evan with a distinct advantage when it came to ODP selection. He was born January 5, which made him the oldest player within the ODP calendar-year age group. He was readily selected to the Maryland State ODP team the two years he tried out. In contrast, travel-team players with August and September birthdays had the natural age advantage—at least until the adults changed the rules. Some sports, particularly those with a high school rather than travel-team focus (think football and wrestling), may be more concerned with the school calendar year. Some sports-crazed parents even hold their kids back an academic year so their older athletes are more physically developed and competitive in high school play. This is no different than redshirting and playing fifth- and sixth-year seniors in college.

In its 2015 policy changes, U.S. Soccer fixed this school-year versus calendar-year age bracket disparity, but the adults again mucked up the transition. U.S. Soccer provided two years' notice regarding the change but erred in failing to implement grandfathering for older age bracket teams in which all players had already been sorted and rostered appropriately. The adults caused a second and totally unnecessary two more years of roster chaos nationally as players and rosters had to again be re-sorted when this change was implemented in 2016–17.

Just like at U12/U13, solid teams again crashed and burned, and players everywhere were displaced. Aggressive team hoppers with birthdays from January to July sought new stronger teams in the younger calendar-year age bracket, while players with birthdays from August to December had to find older calendar-year teams or drop out. Many teams kept the same school-year roster and moved their age group to play up in the older calendar-year bracket. Evan's Fury travel team was one of those that chose to stay together and move up an age group from U16 to U18, skipping U17. Most of the team were high school juniors effectively playing college-bound seniors. More critically, for hundreds of thousands of both girl and boy players, this restructuring occurred during their junior- to senior-year transition and right in the midst of their college recruiting period (2016–17). The pandemic sports shutdowns of 2020 and 2021 caused similar recruiting challenges for juniors and seniors impacted in that timeframe.

Adults Fumble the Ball

Another widely ostracized, adult-implemented policy occurred in February 2012 when U.S. Soccer pronounced that the development academy players (nominally the highest youth level of perhaps one percent of players) would no longer be allowed to play on their high-school teams. The Development Academy level was similar to AAU in basketball or Single A in baseball. U.S. Soccer promoted this policy change ostensibly to develop advanced players and enhance international competitiveness (note that the U.S.

didn't qualify for the World Cup five years later). For Evan and most of his teammates, it instantly ended any interest in the Development Academy system.

The Development Academy eventually allowed waivers and exceptions for kids attending private high schools to creep in. That, of course, provided a natural impetus for soccer players to seek out private school opportunities either for more playing time or exposure. This likely resulted in non-ideal commuting challenges and (pay-to-play) costs for families who were able to go down this path. If an exception for one group, why not all?

I believe the North American system is basically challenged to compete against players from international countries who grow up in a soccer culture and who practice *daily* starting as young as age eight. The U.S. youth soccer system of two practices and a game each week may never compete with daily play and organized professional training up to ten times per week.

Here's what Christian Pulisic, in his November 2017 online article, "1,834 Days," posted to *The Players' Tribune*, had to say on the subject:

In Europe, the average level of ability around you is just so much higher. It's a pool of players where everyone ... is fighting for a spot—truly week in and week out. Which makes the intensity and humility that you need to bring to the field every day ... just unlike anything that you can really experience in U.S. developmental soccer.

In other words, the U.S./Canada school-based athletic systems are unlikely to match Europe's professionalized soccer systems for development.

The North American high school and college focused sports systems have academics as their primary mission, an approach that serves the 99 percent of the eight million U.S. high school athletes more appropriately. Many North American sports (baseball, hockey, basketball and to an extent, soccer) have a well-developed minor league system which kicks in after high school or college. Those super-elite soccer players who aspire to international levels of play may simply have to move to Europe as many top young players have recently done. For the rest, the schooling focus vastly improves future employment prospects as compared to a mainly sports focus.

Break Out the Checkbook

One of the bigger adult-rendered flubs that impacted Evan's sports and academic careers occurred during his freshman year. Evan matriculated at DeMatha Catholic High School, a private school that promotes and actively recruits for advanced sports. DeMatha sports are often ranked nationally; its soccer team finished the 2013 season ranked number one. DeMatha had a well-respected and much-revered coach of more than a decade who had been extremely successful placing players on college teams.

We turned to DeMatha for Evan's soccer play because it seemed to provide the perfect opportunity to play at a near-academy level, learn from a well-regarded coach, and still have the benefits of playing on a high school team. And it *was* perfect, until Coach D botched the well-oiled system he'd developed.

Coach D initiated a travel-team program for the school's players, with a stated intention to mirror a European academy-like system. He set up two freshman teams that required about thirty-six players out of a total freshman class of about 200. That mandated taking on players who had not even played organized soccer before. Realistically, DeMatha had perhaps seven high-quality players per class from which the roster could be developed for its excellent varsity team. Coach D's supplemental travel-team concept was clearly numerically unsustainable in delivering academy-level play.

While playing on Coach D's travel team was not technically mandatory, any player hoping to play on DeMatha's high school team realistically had to join. This new travel team was blatant pay (for the travel team) to play (on the high school team) [==].

Most high school leagues prohibit coaches from coaching players outside the school environment to avoid these kinds of pay-for-play conflicts, and DeMatha's league was no exception. Despite these rules, workarounds (cheating), such as using assistant coaches, spouses, buddies, or the real coach observing from the hill, abound. Is there anyone who hasn't seen an ejected professional coach phoning in instructions from up in the stands? Of course, the league found out about the travel team and ejected the high school team from the league (it was later reinstated, but the long-term coach ended up leaving).

Evan had continued playing on both his Fury and this school-sponsored travel team but quit this new travel team just before the high school league eligibility chaos erupted near the end of freshman year. We had other challenges with this high school, including high cost, a lengthy commute, and a teaching style that wasn't ideal for Evan, particularly when it came to the sciences. We were already working on Evan transferring to a high school with an engineering program and a good soccer team when the travel-team fiasco became the final nail in the coffin for us. We fortunately had the wherewithal (energy and finances) to undertake a family move for an improved academic and sports situation, but we would not have undertaken such drastic actions for a sports-only situation.

State of Play and Pay

Another example of adult gatekeepers running amuck with youth sports appears in the costs related to the strictly managed rules for the annual State Cup championship for travel teams.

First, the *entire* team must show up more than an hour before the games to undergo a mandatory check-in. The prime purpose of this process seemed to be a rigorous and petty uniform inspection. Uniform color, numbers, and matching compliance "will be strictly enforced." That included the color of cold-weather undergarments, including any visible underwear, and compression gear must be color matched. No joke, the requirement for "matching underwear" is written into the youth rules. Even shin guard stays, the holding straps around the socks, must exactly color match. I understand the importance that opposing team jerseys being of contrasting colors, but demanding that players purchase two sets of undergear that exactly match their two (light and dark) uniforms does nothing but add unnecessary costs to youth sports [==].

Another problem with the State Cup rules for U15 through U19 play is that they do not allow for free substitution of players. Any player subbed out cannot return to play during that same half. State Cups are one of the few youth formats, in addition to SuperY and Development Academy, that do not allow free substitution. Even college rules are less restrictive. Without free substitution, starters remain in the game until exhaustion sets in, and substitutes remain benched until the final few minutes of a half; sometimes they're left out for the entire game. Coaches have also been known to retain one stronger player on the bench until the last minutes of a half just in case of injury to one of the key starters.

The lack of free substitution serves to hinder sensible rotation of game minutes and utilization of available youth players [==]. Soccer isn't the only sport with this problem. Some youth baseball leagues also limit free substitution. While limited substitution is fine in professional sports, it does nothing to promote ideal youth participation. In fact, these rules can even result in detrimental impacts, such as stronger players continuing to play while injured to avoid being permanently subbed out.

A final concern with the State Cup is that it is one of the most expensive tournament venues in youth soccer, starting with a $565 application fee and referee fee of $175 per game. Since the State Cup is a single-elimination tournament, half the teams pay $740, or $41 per player for just one game. Along with the State ODP supplemental travel-team system, the State Cup is the poster child for locally based pay-to-play systems. The one offsetting benefit is that these games take place within the player's state. At the extreme other end of the spectrum, the travel team participated in one national-level Disney showcase that cost on the order of $1,000 per game, pay-to-play on steroids.

Balancing Act

These are some of the readily articulated examples I witnessed in which adult organizers and coaches botched various youth sports experiences. We consistently worked to circumvent the negative consequences throughout Evan's journey, and his determination and love of the game helped him overcome many of these challenges. But lots of parents don't have the time, money, or resolve, and many players don't have the same drive or patience to overcome the adult-imposed structural issues. All in all, I believe these types of roadblocks are strong contributors to the reasons why 75 percent of kids drop out of youth sports by their early teens.

Chapter 10

Bigger Fields, Higher Nets, and Deeper Commitments (U15)

Except for a few athletically gifted players, most ordinary kids must make their decision and commitment to the highest potential level of sports they plan to pursue by ages twelve to thirteen when in middle school [==]. From this point forward, how their games are played changes significantly.

In soccer, baseball, and softball, the games transition to full-field play. In basketball, players adjust to ten-foot hoops and full-size balls. In volleyball, this is when players encounter full-height nets, and in football, the change is from flag or weight-based leagues to full-side tackle leagues. By age fourteen (U15), most athletes are well slotted into buckets of development and potential and, in addition, have transitioned to high school play for their freshman year.

Having kids commit to their sports paths as young as age twelve is a big ask; most will not be able to pursue alternatives from here. This commitment also requires full parental support not only in covering costs, but in more commuting to practices and games. In effect, the entire family must commit to this rather exclusive sports journey for the foreseeable future, and that's something that locks out other family commitments.

Youth athletes experience plenty of pressure to make these commitments. Sports organizations, leagues, levels, coaches, and teams are constantly pushing kids to fully commit to their sport as they need their numbers to be sustainable and, of course, they need or want the money. As a result, the information and brochures provided by organizers regularly stretch likely high school, travel team and collegiate outcomes. These are the realities for youth sports at elite levels, and especially for the ordinary kids attempting to reach stretch goals.

I am sure some pundits may question my view that the majority of athletes must select their specialization and desired level of ultimate play at relatively early ages. While examples of athletes who blossomed at later ages exist (Michael Jordan is one), late bloomers are the exception rather than the norm. This may be particularly true for sports in which it takes years of fine and repetitive motor skill development (soccer, baseball, field hockey, lacrosse, tennis, golf, volleyball, and the like), in addition to physical development, to become competent.

Youth teams and rosters are constantly shuffling the deck in search of a special little superstar. The Fury team's turnover of at least thirty-three players is a prime example of this. As the athletes age, the potential to move up a level of play diminishes greatly due to experience, skilled touch, pace, and speed of play becoming more challenging at each level ascended. Just as in academics, work, and life in general, the road to advancement narrows the further you climb.

Is Being an All-Star Worth It?

While on the Maryland State ODP team, Evan was encouraged to try out for a top academy-level organization called Baltimore Celtic. Their teams claimed multiple national championships at different age groups, and joining its roster would have transformed Evan's sports paradigm. While competitive with the team's weakest players, he and I assessed that his chances to obtain meaningful playing time might take a year of development. The rush-hour commutes to two tryouts were ninety minutes each way, and even Evan acknowledged that the commuting situation was going to be a problem with his school schedule. He also didn't want to ride the bench for extended months, because he had already been there, done that. We advised the coach that Evan was opting out before the final tryout session.

Three local peers of Evan's did jump to Celtic despite their excessive commutes. These three athletes all had amazing youth-sports journeys at a higher level of play than the Fury team provided; I believe two won a couple of national championships. Celtic also regularly crushed Evan's teams over the years, though he and his teammates did amazingly eke out a scrimmage tie once and came heartbreakingly close to a second tie in league play. The three Celtic players who were Evan's peers were able to enhance their abilities, but it didn't lead to collegiate stardom. They ended up committing to colleges known more for academics than sports, a not much different outcome than Evan's teammates who also elected to play in college.

How the Good Get Great

The one thing those Celtic tryouts demonstrated was how the organization's players got to be so good. Half of their practice time was spent on fundamental skills development, something that involved *thousands* of foot-touches for each player in the first hour. The players formed two opposing lines, with one ball for each pair of players. Each player touched the ball every few seconds during the drills, which emphasized different kinds of touches to either foot thanks to numerous cones set out to change the touch skill or distance. It was equivalent to a basketball team undertaking shooting practice with multiple balls and nets, a baseball team spending hours in multiple batting cages, a volleyball team practicing two-versus-two drills, or a field hockey team performing one-versus-one passing drills over and over again.

Celtic did not perform drills that used either a single line or numerous players chasing a single ball. Most drills were structured to include a time, pressure, or quantity element meant to maintain an advanced pace of play, not unlike a very tight baseball "pepper" drill. Celtic coaches also used small fields for game-play practice to compress the space and time, the equivalent of a one-quarter court basketball practice.

What the Celtic practices did not seem to focus on much were traditional tactics such as formations, set plays, positioning, triangles, or strategy. They didn't need to. The players naturally excelled at tactics due to their superior ball control.

Evan left his two tryouts with the team exhausted but with a huge smile. He still says, eight years later, that they were "the best practices ever." Though we had decided that joining the team wasn't a good fit for our family, those tryouts confirmed that our focus on supplemental training to improve basic foot skills had been the correct approach all along.

I'm surprised that other coaches never scouted Celtic's practices as the team's focus on basic skills development was unlike any other we encountered. Coaches attend all kinds of certifications to get A- through G-level coaching licenses, but a coach could have learned a lot by simply watching how an exceptional organization runs its practices. I did. In my opinion, Celtic's practices were the best I had observed, yet I never once heard of any local coach who watched or copied its methods [==]. The only other similar practice regimen I witnessed occurred in our local Development Academy program of D.C. United and which Evan experienced through participation in a couple of its camps.

I've grown to realize that either as a parent or coach, we always need to learn more. If I were to do it again, I'd probably go one step further and try to observe more team practices run by the best coaches in the business; 80 percent of sports activities occur at practices, not games. While some practices are closed, others are readily accessible. More than a few coaches have written "how-to" books, but text isn't the same as seeing the action and observing the coaching interactions and intensity. YouTube has videos of open practices for some of the most successful coaches, and, as well, some coaches sell videos of their practice methods (Coach K [Krzyzewski] of Duke is one example). Coaches and coaching end up being the key components of any youth-sports journey.

We skipped ODP at age fourteen but gave it another run at fifteen. Mother Nature conspired against ODP that year, with the February tournament snowed out and four practices canceled due to spring thunderstorms. Nothing is more disheartening to a kid than driving halfway across the state to a cancelled practice, a complete waste of three hours. That year, ODP scheduled about ten practices and a few games with what I'll say was somewhat indifferent—OK, lousy, going-through-the motions coaching for its $1,500 fee plus travel and hotel costs. The ODP state uniforms and the recognition were great, but the high cost and exhaustive commuting time did not make it a good value.

As indicated in the previous chapter, we had also tried to secure higher-level soccer play for Evan by having him attend the all-boys DeMatha High School as a freshman. Since DeMatha turned out to be a less-than-ideal academic fit, we looked for a high school with a stronger STEM-based program. With that transition, *travel* sports took on a new and by far their biggest meaning to our family to date.

We completely uprooted the family and moved twenty-two miles to Severna Park in June 2015. This involved renting a house for three years, renting a U-Haul moving truck, buying a houseful of dumpy Craigslist furniture, renting out our old house, and everything else that goes along with a complete change of address. At one tournament, Evan made me park far away to hide the beat-up Craigslist couch tied to our minivan's roof. We also passed the surveillance test by the school's residency police, which we later learned had double-checked our change in physical homes to ensure we hadn't acquired a false drop box address.

This uprooting was, ostensibly, academically grounded in Severna Park High School's excellent pre-engineering program. Of course, the new soccer coach was advised the move was undertaken in order for Evan to play under his superior tutelage and with his longtime travel teammates. Evan will attest, sometimes with a straight face, that the transfer was not for the better academics, soccer situation, or coaching at all, but rather due to the fact his new school had girls.

The Only Thing Permanent is Change

I am certain the youth structure at the highest levels in the U.S. will be restructured again and again—probably right after this book's publication. Development Academy may no longer be the so-called highest youth level of play. I wouldn't be surprised to see a "Global Academy" with play scheduled in Europe, Mexico, or South America, and who knows what could come after that.

I wrote that last paragraph in 2018, and sure enough, in April 2020, U.S. Soccer abruptly terminated the Development Academy program after thirteen years. It claimed the closure was due to pandemic-related funding challenges. While on the surface this seemed to be a disaster for youth soccer, two high-level organizers immediately stepped in to fill the void, the Major League Soccer (MLS) system that had been a part of the Development Academy, and the Elite Clubs National League.

Still, the fundamental youth-sports systems remain in place, and with each adult-mandated restructuring, athletes get yanked around, have to find a new home, and write additional checks. The organizational structures, level names, and relative commitments (time and money) may change, but the U.S. youth-sports industrial complex will always forever march forward.

Just before our move, the Fury travel team competed in NCSL's Division 1 during the spring of 2015 and finished a respectable third with a 6–3–0 record. Fury also competed in Division 2 of EDP and was the runner-up with a 7–0–1 record. Evan remained slotted on his travel and new high school teams that best fit his athletic abilities and academic interests—and our family's move was about to put the journey back on track for his final three years of youth sports.

Chapter 11

Coaches: The Good, the Bad, and the Yellers

By my count, Evan had thirty-two different coaches over the last twelve years of his journey. On average, that amounted to three different coaches each year, excluding the occasional substitute or guest coaches (Appendix I). The utopian model would be to find the right coach for your kid and stick with that coach for the entire journey, but youth sports don't work like that. The variables of tryout selection, ability progression, physical development, the ability to travel further with age, travel versus high school play, coaching skills, tryout selection politics, and costs all contribute to coaching change-over.

In the peewee years, kids may have different coaches in each fall and spring season. These coaches are typically mom or dad volunteers who have been suckered into coaching. Most have limited if any professional coaching or sports qualifications; I speak with authority on this as the tournament "coach" who had never played one minute of soccer.

At the peewee level of all sports, the primary qualification one seeks in a coach is patience. The technical requirements are to manage practices and keep it fun. Plenty of books and websites provide adequate guidance on how to run youth practices in any sport.

Despite Evan not only surviving but thriving on a parent-coached team, I would recommend avoiding such arrangements beyond the peewee years. Seriousness about playing time and skills development ramps up in the U12 to U14 timeframe, and by then, parental favoritism on the field is best ended.

In the middle years, different coaches serve various purposes, from working with secondary teams, providing supplemental training, and leading school, travel and state teams. Evan was not a serial team hopper, preferring to stay on the same travel team for seven years, unusual in youth soccer. Serial team hoppers or kids who utilize specialized supplemental trainers (batting, shooting, pitching, running, skating, receiving, or conditioning coaches), may end up with many more coaches than Evan did. A few athletes we knew constantly changed teams in search of some nirvana or greener grass, but I always sensed these situations were mostly parent-induced. Most kids prefer a steady sports situation, one where the fit feels good.

Nonetheless, with thirty-two coaches, Evan and his buddies experienced the gamut of skills, likeability, and success. A few were great, the kind of coach who instilled more in the athletes than just running practices and selecting game rosters. The majority of coaches were solid and helped kids progress their game. There were also a few who had good intentions but did not manage players, communications, and games very well [==]. And, like most athletes, Evan encountered a couple of yellers, those coaches who felt duty bound to overcoach and scream out directives for every aspect of the athletes' and team's play. I'll highlight some of the very best and a couple of the challenged coaches.

> "A good coach can change a game. A great coach can change a life." —John Wooden, UCLA basketball coach and ten-time national champion

The Good

The first great coach was Coach Larry, who led the U8 Hurricanes. Coach Larry took on the kids no other coach wanted. He mentored several teams of misfits, including our weak batch of pickup seven-year-olds. Coach Larry wasn't just the ultimate volunteer, he was the first coach who was able to instill a sense of positioning discipline and a defensive mindset in his ragtag group. His often-repeated mantra was, "If they don't score, they can't win" which the team embraced.

Surprisingly, the team ended up with just one loss and went on to become the Spring 2008 runner-up. These positive results were, in part, thanks to Coach Larry bringing along his highly skilled and tough daughter Jess to the team, much to all the boys' initial lament. Eventually, the teammates came to enjoy making successful outlet passes to scoring threat Jess. To this day, Evan will only admit to favoring passes to Jess because of assists, but I believe all the boys liked passing to Jess because they all grew to like her and appreciated her strong play as the team's clear scoring hero.

The next great coach was the U10 Red Storm's Coach John (not me). Coach John was outwardly a tough guy, which is exactly what disorganized, ten-year-old wannabe athletes need. Coach John imparted firm, military-like discipline with the boys, at times having the players do push-ups or run laps when they misbehaved.

Coach John was the father of Evan's teammate Joe, but Joe did not benefit from this. Unlike most coaching parents, Coach John was blatantly tougher on Joe than any other team member. In fact, I think Joe spent a couple of practices mainly doing push-ups or laps instead of kicking a ball. Coach John's toughness was probably a function of his military background, and he was equally tough on his other children, all of whom played soccer and lacrosse with success.

Coach John was the first we knew who had total team control and accepted zero parental intervention from the sidelines. He was, effectively, Evan's first real "big boy" coach. He also took no bull from the referees. One time, Coach John was profusely expressing sympathy about a questionable call with his Red Storm players. When the referee marched over and was just about to yank out a yellow card, Coach John loudly but calmly responded by putting his arm around one of the field players and stating, "I am talking to my man! Can't a coach talk to his men?" The referee was so taken aback by having nine- and ten-year-olds referred to as "men" he about-faced and kept the card in his pocket.

Coach John managed the players with an approach of maturity beyond their years. He was also the first coach to take the team to the woodshed at halftime or after a game when the team's effort had been less than stellar. He cared more about effort than the score, a rarity among youth coaches.

I have no idea what Coach John said to the boys following these times of poor performance, as he marched the team well out of parental earshot. When I'd ask Evan what had been said to the team, all I could get out of him was, "Coach might have used some bad words." As a measure of his total respect for Coach John, he has never confessed what those bad words might have been. It was strictly between coach and the boys.

Supplemental Coach Nate from SoccerMeansMore was certainly Evan's best skills-based coach as a detailed student of the game and a meticulous observer of individual player abilities, strengths, and weaknesses. He articulated soccer finesse, translated it into finely skilled moves, and facilitated development. He also positively mentored each player's mental conditioning. It was our loss that Coach Nate was destined to move on to collegiate coaching. Finding a coach with his level of personal focus is terribly uncommon. I often wonder how well Evan's skills might have improved with five years of Coach Nate's supplemental training instead of just two.

The Bad

Many of the earlier coaches we worked with were fathers of a player. Coach John was the only coach outwardly tougher on his own son than the other teammates. Poor Joe. Most coaches who were player parents handled their sons largely in an appropriate manner. A few may have squeezed in a few extra playing minutes for their kid, but I felt this was justified in exchange for their time commitment. Kudos to those who did not show unwarranted favoritism, including Coaches Peter, Jeff, Roger, Milko, Frank, Mike M, Jason, Tom, Doug, and Tim.

Coach B, on the other hand, was the type of parent who managed the team's play seemingly for the benefit of his child [==]. His game objective was to ensure his son played every minute as *the* striker, assigned to take all corner and free kicks and taking most throw-ins. In essence, he was staged to be the team hero. I am sure my memory is biased, but Coach B seemed to find fault—and, granted, this lousy team had *plenty* of fault—with every other kid's play. The generic term for this behavior is "Daddy Ball." (There's no gender-equivalent term for mom coaches, perhaps due to a reduced proclivity toward favoritism.)

Coach K was another who exhibited blatant favoritism toward his son. In the early years, he made sure his son took all the free kicks, penalty kicks, and throw-ins. Sometimes the game took a commercial-length time-out as the teams waited for Coach K's son to hustle from one end of the field to the other. Once the game shifted to the full-field size, Coach K sensibly abandoned the requirement his son take all throw-ins.

Coach K also exhibited favoritism to his son's long-term buddies who'd grown up in the same town. The son's clique often received extra playing time, special attention, and probably some sense of entitlement [==] relative to those who grew up elsewhere.

Evan was the team's first recruit who hadn't grown up in Coach K's town, and so he became the first team member to have to work through Clique Leader K's coaching issues. In the early years on this team, Evan endured more than his fair share of bench time. While this was somewhat due to his pace, I believe Coach K's propensity to favor his locals, even the slower ones, was also a factor. Fortunately, Evan's improved playing and his constant commitment remedied this issue—he attended more practices and games than any other team member over the seven years—but the issue extended to other non-locals who, at times, also seemed parked on the bench when their abilities or effort should have put them on the field. Over the years, new players tried out, new players came, and new players left. At least thirty-three different kids left the team over those seven years (Appendix I), and I feel that Coach K's favoritism toward his six core local players likely contributed to this revolving door.

The unbalanced playing time did not foster team camaraderie. I suspect all youth teams have an underlying schism between long-term starters and new bench players regardless whether those starters are sourced from the local community. But it took Evan about three years to be fully accepted and integrated by the travel team, and I'd venture to say he was never universally accepted by his later high school locals despite playing varsity for three years. The small Severna Park clique of long-term locals was powerful in both travel and high school soccer, and many other players that joined the team never broke into their inner circle.

As the long-term outsider, Evan readily identified with the challenges of team integration and, as a result, often helped out new teammates during practices. Frankly, he never cared much about cliques, even outside of sports. The only two issues that *would* aggravate Evan were if a player tried to boss him around or was demonstrably lazy by not working to get open or help with defensive coverage. Fortunately, all coaches (and players) were aligned on these two issues. Bossy kids were generally shut down, and lazy players always ended up falling by the wayside.

I suspect Coach K, to this day, may be unaware of his biases, but a few examples can show how coaches like this provide serious obstacles for kids. In the early years with the team, if some of the less favored players, including Evan, made one mistake, they might get yanked from the game and benched. This occurs in all youth sports. On a few of these occasions, Coach K even directly said to Evan, "You should play like my son." In at least two instances that I overheard, I noticed that his son then screwed up far worse, several times in a row, yet was neither benched nor reprimanded for his imperfect play. Those were probably the most hurtful words Evan encountered from any coach throughout his journey, and the scenario played out several times early in his journey with this team. Ouch!

Such negative feedback never helped any player's confidence, but coaches nitpicking the play of those they don't favor is common in youth sports as a way to justify the benchings for some and extra playing time for others.

I observed this kind of treatment with many players on a variety of teams, and my daughter and her cohorts experienced it in other sports. In a few cases, if these kinds of adult interactions occurred in activities outside of "tough" sports, these coaches might even be called out for bullying. Sometimes, the kids had no choice but to suck it up because raising a stink or quitting was a losing proposition. Fortunately, Coach's K's interactions with the kids improved a lot over time, and Evan simply moved beyond any issues to the extent he looks upon Coach K quite favorably in retrospect.

Still, his player management was never totally evenhanded and stalwarts like Evan benefitted. During this time, the travel team had acquired a strong defender from the next town over. This defender played consistently well and had been successfully utilized when some of the favorites were playing baseball. But when the locals returned, this player was parked on the bench. In one tournament game, he didn't play a single minute despite ample opportunity. What's the inevitable outcome when an All-County player receives zero minutes of play on a travel team? That player walks and finds a new team.

Similarly, in a tough Maryland State Cup playoff game, three of the team's favored locals hadn't practiced in recent weeks, thanks to spring baseball. Yet the locals started, while several more sharply tuned players, including regular Evan, started on the bench. The team was completely overrun during the first twenty minutes of play, and conceded what turned out to be the lone, losing goal. Coach K, to his credit, promptly adjusted the lineup to put his more practiced players on the field, but it was already too late as the other team had switched to park-the-bus mode.

Perhaps the most egregious example of inappropriate playing time I witnessed was for a player who traveled with the team to Pittsburgh, Pennsylvania, for a pair of weekend games. This player committed his entire weekend, ten-plus hours of car travel, and the costs for a hotel and meals for just five minutes playing time in only one of the two games. That player left the team soon after, and that left an indelible mark on the team. Local or not, a lot of players didn't like seeing a teammate get totally shafted.

Lastly, at a few away tournaments, Coach "Clique Leader" and some fellow clique parents and players didn't stay at the team's designated hotel, instead booking rooms together in a different hotel. Likewise, they regularly skipped the team dinners at these tournaments, opting to do their own thing. Separating like this would have been fine if finances were a problem, but this group usually upscaled the hotels and undertook their own aftergame activities. Meanwhile, those in the team hotel went to the pool together, watched EPL games together, and played hall soccer together—exactly as it should be. I personally found it particularly odd for a select clique, led by one of the coaches, to purposely avoid team camaraderie activities while traveling.

The Yellers

The first yeller was Coach B on the rising U12 team [==]. Evan joined this team because Coach B had an excellent soccer pedigree, and the team was accepted into the NCSL league, a major step up in the level of play.

Coach B's game management is what fed his frustration and vocal antics. For example, he played the weakest, slowest players as the team's two defensive fullbacks. He then played steady, disciplined, but not quick Evan as the central sweeper in a three-back defensive line in eight-versus-eight play. Evan was constantly yelled at for not instantly transporting himself *Star Trek*-like from sideline to sideline to compensate for the two fullbacks completely overrun on either flank.

It didn't take long before we started shopping for a new team, long before the end of Coach B's "perfect season" of nine straight crushing yell-fests. While we believe he had decent intentions, he just was not a good coach from the management of the kids to communications with the parents. It was Evan's only completely disastrous season. It lasted just a couple of months in the fall of 2011, and Coach B's tenure on the field did not last much longer.

Interestingly, six years later, I ended up sitting in the stands within yelling distance of Coach B when his son's high school team was playing Evan's. His son's team played to the best of its ability, but its players were overmatched. The final score was 8–1. I can confirm with good authority, once a yeller, always a yeller.

Coaches yelling at or intimidating youth athletes is never ideal.

Coach K, the Fury assistant coach for Evan's seven years, was another consistent yeller. Paired with Coach Kenny, the nominal head coach who had a calm, smooth demeanor, they were a classic Jekyll and Hyde/ Good Cop-Bad Cop pairing.

Remarkably, that dichotomy seemed to work. One time, the team was playing a U15 tournament game in North Carolina, but Coach K had been unable to attend. The team's play was lackluster through the first half. During halftime, Evan commented, "Maybe we'd be playing better if Coach K were here to yell at us." This brought huge team laughs and much improved second-half play.

> "Organized sports have become a fertile ground for coaches with bulging veins, foul mouths, clenched fists, and volatile tempers." —Fred Engh, founder, National Alliance for Youth Sports, and a leading youth sports advocate

Still, I'd recommend against having kids play for a yeller despite Evan's game progressing well in this environment. Yes, there is a line between yelling for encouragement and intimidation or abuse. I regularly saw team environments that were so toxic with bullying that leaving would be the only sane option. As bad as those situations were, none compared to the challenges faced by elite gymnasts over the past thirty years, a sport that's been the poster child for abusive approaches to youth athlete success. I marvel that so many kids take it and keep going.

The uneven handling of players by coaches is pervasive, but I don't think most coaches notice their communication issues or biases. In this regard, sports parallel life, where authority figures in school and work are constantly evaluating others, but not necessarily in an equitable or balanced way. People generally deal with it or move on. Still, no one condones tough coaching to the extent of abuse with kids; it can cause permanent issues. In sports, a fine line exists between gritty toughness and abuse—Bobby Knight comes to mind as coach who won championships, yet threw chairs. For children in youth sports, dealing with inconsistent coaches and going on to thrive is an early introduction to these life lessons.

The Game Changer

With just four short months to go in his youth-sports journey, I thought Evan had experienced the gamut of coaching extremes and was finished dealing with new coaches. I was wrong.

When his travel team of seven years crashed due to a terminal case of senioritis, we scrambled to find an alternative team. Evan joined Juventus (Juve) and Coach Pat without a tryout or even a meeting. Evan was selected solely on word-of-mouth credentials, and two days later, he was playing. He knew the names of only two of his teammates.

In that first game, Coach Pat subbed in a couple of other players and Evan after about eighteen minutes, more than fair treatment of a total newbie the Coach had not yet seen play. Evan's initial play was solid, but after about eight minutes, he uncharacteristically turned right into pressure and nervously gave up the ball twice in a row. I waited for the things that never came: *What?!* No yelling by the coach? No being yanked off the field? No screaming about what he should do to correct his play? This was *not* youth coaching as I had come to know it.

Two minutes later, Evan performed a strong move, and Coach Pat instantly bellowed, "Good job, Evan!" A few minutes later, Evan executed an excellent tackle, followed by a nice through-ball pass, and the coach again yelled, "Excellent, Evan!" And then I noticed that Coach Pat regularly yelled out positive accolades to every player whenever they performed well, whether that player was a longtime starter or newbie Evan—and he did *not* yell out a bunch of corrective, micromanaging directives typical of so many youth coaches.

Evan was subbed off the field after an eighteen-minute shift, right along with the regulars. Could I believe what I was seeing? Coach Pat was distributing playing time to achieve the best balance of fresh legs, without regard to cliques, favoritism, or limiting a newbie's minutes? His player rotations weren't just fair, they were well managed.

Evan was increasingly utilized in the second half, and as his nervousness started to wear off; he started playing like himself. The team was barely holding on to a 2–1 lead in a tight battle. In the closing twelve minutes, Coach Pat, in a surprising move, sent Evan to the critical holding midfielder position to park the bus and close out the win. We had never seen a coach do that with a new player, let alone one who'd had a couple of nervous mistakes in his first shift.

I came to genuinely appreciate Coach Pat, as he was always positive with the players. In one game, a player messed up several times, which led to a bit of on-field bickering with another teammate. The postgame chat was all about winning and losing *as a team*, and no player or incident was named. Coach Pat admonished that, regardless the score or situation, Juve would strive to play as a team. I was blown away.

Coach Pat also performed an amazing public service for the players' parents. Sometime during the season, he'd taken it upon himself to monitor all the team's social media (Instagram, Snapchat, Facebook, etc.) activities. After one practice, Coach Pat counseled all the players after he'd observed negative posts using foul language, belittling opponents, and utilizing demeaning language towards high school rivals. He then ordered all offending posts be removed to prevent college recruiting efforts being compromised.

This wasn't an issue for Evan, as we had already browbeaten our kids about negative social media posts, but we were thrilled that Coach Pat's independent mentorship would have a positive reinforcing effect on the whole team.

The impact of positive coaching and a lack of negative consequences for mistakes saw Evan starting to move the needle again as a player. He felt the freedom to play his best rather than play to mainly avoid mistakes. Sure, mistakes also increased a little, and his excellent Juve teammates covered, but his instances of aggressive defensive plays and stepping in front of opponents to steal balls shot up tremendously.

The other outcome from Coach Pat's relentlessly positive style was that many teammates similarly provided encouraging comments and recognition of fellow teammates who made spectacular plays. This level of teammate encouragement was a totally new experience for us all. This environment resulted in excellent team chemistry, and Evan felt like he was just "one of the boys" after only a couple of months. Simply put, soccer was *fun* again.

Chapter 12

Recruiting Videos—Don't Believe the Hype (U16)

Summer 2015 should have been the joyous start to the final chapters of Evan's elite youth-sports journey and college recruiting exploits. Instead, our family was relegated, not to the lower league, but to box hell. We moved out of our house and prepped it for a furnished rental. Meanwhile, we were madly buying cheap Craigslist furniture for our new rental house. At the same time, my job transferred to Texas, and I moved there on "bachelor" status. Then my father passed away, and amidst all the chaos of moving and partially relocating across the country, we had to sort out his house and many possessions.

All the while, youth sports never, ever stopped. Evan attended three ID soccer camps, plus two engineering camps at targeted colleges. He also ramped up supplemental training in preparation for the upcoming sophomore season at his new high school. He was ready, as were his travel teammates. The high school coach was not.

Change-Up

Evan managed the transition to his new high school and engineering program well, but he and his fellow sophomores were mostly consigned to the bench; nine of the travel-team sophomores were as good or better than many juniors and seniors. High school and college coaches have the increased challenge of managing playing time for roughly twenty-eight players on their rosters, something far more difficult than managing a travel team's eighteen players. A similar juggling act occurs for high school football, lacrosse, basketball, field hockey, baseball, and softball teams. The large roster issue can be particularly problematic at schools that have implemented a no-cut athletic policy. Severna Park sports teams did cut players, but most still had large rosters of solid to excellent players. That contributed to legions of solidly talented kids warming the bench, but many coaches simply favor playing upperclassmen and letting the marginally stronger underclassmen wait their turn.

Evan had the additional burden of being a total newcomer. He was occasionally called a "hop-on," and he could not always tell if this moniker was directed in a joshing or judgmental way. I also sensed a few parents in the tight-knit community harbored some resentment that our family could and would undertake the huge family move for an improved academic and sports situation. But we weren't the first to do this. Other families also moved to Severna Park to gain access to the High School's excellent academics, even when sports weren't a consideration.

That's when we discovered a return to Cliquesville. This may have resulted from the tension caused by adding another quality player competing for limited playing time, which occurs in all sports. It is only natural that established players almost automatically snub new outsiders intruding on their team and taking up roster spots, whether it's the high school or travel team.

During this sophomore season, Evan had one particularly great game in which his team played nine-versus-eleven thanks to two red cards. The nine-man team amazingly pulled off a tie. Following that game, the coach benched all but one of the sophomores for most of the remainder of the season. The high school team racked up one of its weaker seasons at 8–5–1 and was soundly ejected from the playoffs with a 5–1 loss to another middle of the standings team. Evan did see the field in ten games, but barely. *Oh well, maybe next year?*

One benefit Evan received from this first year with his new high school team was that it reaffirmed that all his extra training was paying off. For the first time, the players encountered mandatory timed beep-test interval and distance-running endurance trials. Evan confirmed he was now among the faster players, and his relative speed would continue to improve through the remainder of his journey. This enhanced his playing confidence.

During the Spring 2016 travel season, Evan's Fury travel team moved up to Division 1 of the EDP and Region 1 leagues. The team finished middle of the pack in each, which was respectable given the high level of competition. Several teams had been ranked number one nationally over the years, and one had even won the U.S. Youth National Championship. The Fury team was now consistently ranked in the top 125 nationally.

Fury also played in the top-level Jefferson, Annandale, and Potomac showcase tournaments, where they managed two wins in nine games. Somehow, the coaches convinced the tournament schedulers to place Fury against the country's best teams in the highest bracket. This led to highly competitive soccer but many losses. In one tournament, Fury played three teams ranked in the top twenty-two nationally. Realistically, half the team didn't have the ball-control skills to be competitive with these top teams. The experience was great for development, but perhaps not the best to promote love of the game.

Videos Are a Recruiting Tool, but Not the Tool

Competing against top opponents presented the perfect opportunity to produce the much-touted college recruiting videos. The travel team started filming all games, thanks to super-volunteer mom Chris. All the college recruiting literature recommended developing a highlight reel showing how spectacular little Billy or Susie is. Naïve me didn't know at the time, but sports videos were quite oversold as a recruiting tool, and it is only in hindsight that we realized they weren't an absolute necessity. Having said that, I can envision a growing importance of these videos if socially distanced recruiting becomes a future norm as a result of the pandemic or other issues.

For Evan's era, about the best an unsolicited video might hope to produce was a slight bit of interest, one that might mean, just maybe, a coach might make the time to spend a few minutes watching a player at a showcase tournament. What a recruiting video won't do is prompt a college coach to offer a roster position on the spot.

After recording and downloading each eighty- or ninety-minute game video, it must be completely watched and rewatched to find the few segments that highlight the most spectacular plays. Each four- to nine-second segment must then be clipped and edited out. Once these segments are downloaded, the next step is to add editing via circles, stars, arrows, etc., that clearly identify your player. This identification is critical.

Recruiting videos take significant time and effort to produce [==]. The recruiting video we assembled for Evan, for instance, took about forty-five hours total. I watched hours and hours of games, perhaps fifteen games in total for a total of twenty-two hours of tape time, to capture sixty-two highlights of Evan playing against nine highly ranked teams.

All that was after spending more than a few hours learning to master Hudl.com's editing software. Somewhere in the process, an invisible Google Chrome update tweaked Hudl's editing software to the point that it no longer worked properly. After many hours of Hudl tech support and frustration, I tried Microsoft Explorer, which instantly fixed the problem. This software issue set me back a frustrating five or six hours. Back on track, I still had a couple of hours of editing to add identifying circles, include a not-too-wild music track, and upload the video to YouTube.

Evan's highlight video assembled segments that made him look great on the ball in the midfield—not quite Andrés Iniesta or Kevin DeBruyne but solid. Since the highlight video was posted, I'd guess that all but a handful of views have been by family members and probably a few buddies who want to goof on him. Still, I later went on to make several targeted versions with the content adjusted to appeal to specific queries from interested coaches.

I should acknowledge that Hudl and other video companies do provide an excellent product for all the anxiety-filled, helicopter parents out there. For example, we monitored video view count immediately after Evan sent recruiting emails that included a video link to college coaches. Evan also signed up on the college coaches sports recruiting website. We know seven out of twenty college coaches opened the video link and watched at least portions of the video shortly after being pinged with an email. That is something, but I wouldn't equate a viewing rate of 35 percent as an outstanding success.

"You aren't a recruit until a coach knows about you." —Pat Dolan, St. Cloud State baseball coach

I have come to believe that some college/coaches' website recruiting sign-ups are utilized as much for trolling for paying camp attendee dummies as for actual identification and recruiting of team players. While a few coaches did indeed watch the video, Evan's email or phone did not ring off the hook with follow-up interest. This lack of interest included a couple of targeted NCAA Division III (D3) coaches working at what we'd considered "soccer safety" colleges—they never even clicked on the link.

For anyone who doesn't have the time to develop a video with Hudl or other software, many professional sports video firms now attend most showcase tournaments. I am sure they work with other youth sports as well, as this is a fast-growing segment of professionalized support to youth sports activities.

The challenge with any professional video is the significant time and cost invested. Some sports provide limited true action-time viewing per game with estimates for some as follows: football, eleven minutes; high school baseball, fourteen minutes; and continuous soccer, fifty-eight minutes. Individual players will then have even more limited game-action segments of which half or more could be out of frame, unfocused, or misplayed (turnovers, fouls, fumbles, missed blocks, strikeouts, errors, bad passes, penalties, etc.). Also, each player's action generally lasts only a few seconds, so to develop a several-minute highlight video takes many games for all but the exceptional athlete.

The only recruiting videos I am certain were worthwhile were three we custom-made in direct response to comments provided by three targeted coaches after they'd observed Evan's play at showcase tournaments. Two had indicated they'd liked his midfield play from their limited observations, but they wanted to see more to ensure his play was confident on the ball.

I noted that college coaches often observed an athlete only ten to fifteen minutes at a tournament, something that anyone should understand is insufficient when it comes to assessing a player. This included coaches from small D-III programs for which Evan and his teammates would have been a catch. I was also the Fury and Juventus team representative who handed out the team brochures to interested college coaches at tournaments. In doing so, I was able to talk with a number of these coaches and answer questions about our team and players during the game. These brief one-on-one connections with so many coaches helped me better see the challenges of the recruiting process from their viewpoint.

It's Not Always Your Kid's Day to Shine

Hopes and aspirations aside, coaching assessments during tournament games ended up being a random affair not only for Evan, but all players. What if the coach was assessing a striker and the ball never got to the offensive end of the field? What if the coach had arrived to observe a scouted player but the player was just subbed off the field after his designated shift? These kinds of misses happened to even the best players, and fueled a good amount of parental angst. A couple of times, I even heard parents of opponents begging coaches to hang around and wait for their player to get back into the game.

One targeted college coach observed Evan for one half of a game at a showcase tournament where an overnight monsoon had deposited four inches of rain. The field had become a seabed more suitable to waterskiing than soccer. The few exposed islands remaining above water produced a huge sucking sound whenever players attempted to extract their cleats from the quagmire. The only strategy to be had was to kick all passes airborne. I don't know how he managed it, but Evan completed a number of pinpoint flips from one sludgy mound to another, and, frankly, looked as sharp as any shark in the sea.

Random external variables such as field conditions, coach schedules, or pandemics can hugely impact recruiting success.

The opposite occurred at one ID camp, where the fields resembled a wheat field ready for harvest. Passes along the ground had to be kicked with Superman-like force to mow down a path in the overgrowth. Just as they had on the flooded field, the players again chipped passes in the air to ensure the ball did not become ensnarled or lost in the thick thatch. Players uniformly complained that this camp was obviously more concerned about making money than hosting a serious recruiting assessment.

Evan always preferred artificial turf fields, which offered the advantages of field consistency and did not succumb to weather cancellations. Few youth-level grass fields had sufficient uniformity to enable perfectly weighted through-ball passes, and unevenly tufted fields do not help sharp passers deliver their best qualities. And turf fields never had ticks, something we had in such abundance on one of his early regular-play fields that we developed a postgame, tick-check ritual. The downsides of turf fields were the inevitable and excessive heat generated in the summer sun, and of course, those damnable turf-turd bits.

We were not surprised Evan obtained no traction with either the swamp or wheat-field coach. Those two opportunities vanished due to the horrible field conditions, which could not in any way provide a reasonable assessment of a player's capabilities. Likewise, at one ID camp, Evan came down with pneumonia and amazingly played through it, but his performance suffered. As I write this in 2021, the pandemic virtually stopped the normal assessment and recruiting process for the last eighteen months. Who would have guessed that on-field shift timing, random ball locations, unusual field conditions, coach schedules, public health issues, and temporary injury setbacks are critical variables potentially impacting an athlete's longer-term college opportunities [==]?

The Missing Link

For those two college coaches with specific follow-up questions about Evan's play, we downloaded and forwarded highlights from a game against a highly ranked opponent, where Evan completed an amazing 52 passes at an 88 percent completion rate. In this game, Evan was on the ball in a positive manner six out of his seventy minutes of playing time.

It was a special day for him. In typical games, Evan completed about twenty-five to thirty passes at an average completion rate approaching 80 percent, and he'd be positively on the ball about three-and-a-half minutes. As the main central midfielder, he often led the team in these statistics. Many teammates made just ten to fifteen passes with a completion rate in the 50 to 60 percent range. How do I know all of this? I learned this from watching hours and hours of game videos and recording lots of data.

I now believe Evan's pass completion percentage was far too high for a youth player. His high pass completion numbers were a direct result of being too conservative in pass selection, that conservatism influenced by negative coaching. Evan made passes to retain possession and keep from giving the ball away, something that sometimes resulted in being yelled at or benched.

The game in which Evan completed 52 passes was clearly an outlier to his statistical record—it was probably his best youth game ever. In fact, the statistics were right up there with the best professional midfielders. For the 2016–17 season, the top five English Premier League midfielders (Granit Xhaka, Fernando "Fernandinho" Luiz Roza, Paul Pogba, N'Golo Kanté, and Mesut Özil) completed an average of 57 passes during a ninety-minute game (equivalent to 51 passes in an eighty-minute game) at an 87 percent completion rate, according to statistics downloaded and averaged from the Squawka.com website. Our targeted video did seem to alleviate concerns expressed by the two coaches about Evan's overall passing skills, although he later dropped his interest in these two colleges.

A third coach confirmed he was confident of Evan's strong foot skills and high passing efficiency, but he was "not yet sold on his defensive capabilities." This assessment was based on the coach's observation from one half of play at the end of a three-game tournament that had not the best game played by either Evan or his team. Fortunately, the team had filmed two earlier games that this college's assistant coach had observed.

I downloaded only defensive interventions against the two top sixty teams the assistant coach had observed. Those games showed that Evan had nineteen and fourteen strong tackles or defensive interventions respectively. Interestingly, these defensive stops were higher than his typical twelve to thirteen per game average, and many were against physically big and extremely athletic opponents, a lucky happenstance. This video helped assuage the head coach's concern about Evan's defensive capabilities.

Though we did a solid job of developing these highlight videos from sophomore into junior year, I'm now convinced they weren't really necessary. They didn't open any doors, as the majority of college coaches never watched them. Later discussions with teammates and other sports parents indicated similar observations. Certainly, no coach ever selected an ordinary player based solely on a recruiting video.

While the process of producing the recruiting highlight video lacked the value we hoped for, we did learn one important thing: Instead of focusing on making videos, we should have been *watching* them.

We should have started watching college games of the teams and coaches Evan wanted to target to see if their style of play and coaching were a match. Most college games are streamed live on the web and then posted on the team's website. Unfortunately, we never checked out these resources until the very end of the recruiting process, and by that time, Evan had reduced his choices to just a few colleges. Had we discovered the value in these videos earlier, we not only would have saved time and camp money, but also Evan would have been able to narrow down the colleges and coaches in a much more efficient way.

Chapter 13

Scouting the College Sports Landscape

The first step in the college search is a coordinated effort between high schoolers and their parents to identify potential target colleges. The most critical variables are finding an academic structure, vibe, and career path that fit the student. But with more than three thousand four-year colleges and universities to choose from, the identification and eventual narrowing of the list can seem daunting. For athletes, the increased variables and complexities make the task far more difficult, so families cannot be passive and park the bus.

Finding the Strike Zone

For some reason beginning at an early age, Evan indicated that his ultimate objective was to play sports in college; he never expressed any aspirations for professional sports participation. What he did do, eventually, was refine his hope to maybe play at a D1 college.

I'm sure most high school athletes dream of top-tier D1 without any understanding of the academic or athletic advantages and disadvantages that come along with attendance at a university or college at that tier. Who wouldn't want to play football at Alabama, women's volleyball at Nebraska, women's basketball at UConn, men's basketball at Duke, or women's lacrosse at Maryland?

Knowing that Evan was potentially aiming for such college stature, our first strategy was to help determine which institutions might be a potential fit. With so much worthwhile information readily discoverable on the web, we began our search from the comfort of my Barcalounger, but we didn't go about the search blindly.

We knew that many college coaches focus on credentials. For example, the ID camp final all-star game always consisted of those athletes with the strongest incoming credentials, regardless of how other athletes performed during the camp. This is no different than competition in the workplace, where employees with top-tier college degrees often get the nod over stronger and harder working employees with less prestigious pedigrees.

In truth, Evan didn't have outstanding credentials—lots of goals, a slot on a national or all-state team, etc. Nor was he the child of a movie star competing for one of those special "Varsity Blues" roster spots. So, he was never going to be first in line as a D1 recruit. Like most of his teammates and peers in other sports, Evan was destined to be in the mix of athletes trying for the final spots in D1 or D2 college play or to be a more favored D3 or D-whatever recruit. Acknowledging this reality, Evan, Karen, and I first identified colleges with a solid potential academic and social fit and *then* looked to find a subsequent good athletic fit among that list. Many books and websites are available to help sort and find the right academic fit. We particularly liked the websites collegedata.com and the high school sponsored naviance.com.

Evan provided Karen and I with input on his preferred college type and academic interests. Through high school, he'd participated in a national engineering prep program called Project Lead the Way, a STEM-like program, and determined he would be majoring in mechanical engineering. That helped eliminate perhaps 75 percent of D2 and D3 liberal arts colleges, including several where coaches had expressed specific interest in him (Appendix III). Evan also had a preference for mid-sized colleges, those having at least 2,000 students but less than 15,000, and he knew he wanted to attend college somewhere in the east. With those parameters we were able to narrow his list to about fifty colleges, about half of which were D1.

To support the D1 vision, I performed a sports assessment of all the D1 college programs on our reduced list. I immediately eliminated the most competitive conferences such as the ACC, Big 10, SEC, Pac-12, etc. Evan understood that he was not going to play at these colleges. Even if he could survive as a practice dummy and bench sitter, it would not be the college sports experience he was seeking.

Next, I looked for appropriate conferences and colleges that anyone can research on NCAA.org. These data are available for most college sports and for women's and men's teams. I focused on the final NCAA 2015 RPI rankings to determine which conferences had D1 colleges with programs ranked toward the lower half. Even though we had an intuitive sense for the likely results, we wanted to make sure we didn't overlook any block of potential colleges from our list of 205 with D1 programs. From there, I calculated the average team rankings for the following five conferences: Patriot League (101), Atlantic 10 (134), Colonial (103), America East (87), and Big East (81). The first three conferences have a significant portion of their teams ranked in the lower half of all D1 programs, so they held the best chance of ordinary players fitting in if they could get traction.

The data we pulled revealed other interesting observations. America East's rankings were tightly clustered between 48 and

111, while the Big East's rankings were spread from 7 to 186, with four teams below 120. Of course, no two sports programs are alike, but we could still highlight a potential opportunity even within a losing program. In sharp contrast, the ACC's average ranking was thirty-four, with seven teams in the top twenty-five—we could forget that conference.

Armed with our new list of colleges, we needed to compare which of them offered the desired mechanical engineering program. This got the list down to fifteen potential D1 colleges from the Patriot, Atlantic 10, Colonial, and America East leagues. To these we added another fifteen engineering-focused D3 colleges for a fifty-fifty split in these two divisions. From there, we took a harder look at the academics, evaluating whether the standards were a safe bet or a stretch for admission. We were a little surprised, once we'd taken this harder look, that some of those colleges with weaker academic standards seemed to have more competitive sports teams, which, in the big picture, means that athletes may have to trade off academic and sports standards [==].

Putting the Coaches on Tryout

Additional insights to sports programs and the challenges and bias exhibited by the various coaches can be gained from researching college websites. My investigations quickly eliminated half the college sports programs when we could see that a coaching style was not ideally suited for mere mortal athletes like Evan. Also, nearly all such knowledge can be gleaned without any direct social interaction, which is beneficial for those with cost, time, distance, and even today's pandemic-related challenges. The number one bias we observed was a preference for height and size [==], an issue endemic throughout an athlete's journey from youth through college and in many sports. Evan's 5'9-10" height and 140-pound weight was about average for high school midfielders. In fact, his recruiting brochure height was often a reported tippy-toe half-inch taller and weight a few pounds heavier. He tended to bulk up with weightlifting during the high school offseason and then shed ten pounds as the season progressed with practices and games six days a week. Heck, like any teenage athlete, he could gain several pounds in one dinner sitting and then lose ten pounds over a three-game tournament weekend.

Evan was fundamentally not tall enough for many D1 programs and even one D3 program. I researched height bias and found four colleges had rosters with four or fewer players at 5'9" or shorter; typical D1 rosters have seven to eleven players at 5'9" or shorter. In two cases, the shorter players were European athletes. Two colleges had rosters with an average team height solidly over six feet. I'd say the diminutive professional Christian Pulisic might even have a challenge being recruited by these height-biased programs, let alone Evan!

Bias number two is the use of international athletes [==], something frequently encountered in basketball, tennis, hockey, and baseball. Let's be frank, the best European, African, and South American boys are better at soccer than most Americans. An ODP coach passed on an anecdote about this concerning a Maryland U15 ODP team that traveled to Scotland and played a local U13 academy team. After the older Maryland team got soundly thumped by the Scots, the ODP coach apologized to the Scottish coach for his team's lack of competitiveness. The Scottish coach responded by similarly apologizing that the Scottish U11 team was not available to play.

International collegiate athletes tend to be several years older and more mature than our American-raised youths and, as a result, tend to be stronger athletes. To meet U.S. college academic standards, these student-athletes (or, um, athlete-students) have sometimes spent extra years in overseas or U.S. preparatory schools to hone their SAT and other college entrance qualifications such as English as a second language. One D1 parent advised me the average age of his son's college team was above twenty-three, thanks to its older international athletes. In addition, international players can potentially be eligible for needs-based scholarships, which can circumvent their need for the 9.9 (men's) or 14 (women's) soccer scholarships. International athletes, by definition, also have the advantage of enhancing diversity to any college's student body, which may be looked upon favorably by the admissions staff.

While the presence of international athletes in the collegiate ranks is well known, I doubt most realize how prevalent the issue is in D1 men's soccer. Evan slammed into a brick wall with one of the smaller colleges he'd initially favored. This college had nine internationals, all of whom started, and that didn't leave much room for American players. I then checked his D1 target schools, and immediately eliminated half due to a strong international bias. (D3 college rosters generally have few international athletes.)

Since I hadn't retained my 2015 data analysis, as I started this book in 2017, I recalculated the number of international athletes rostered on the eight D1 colleges we had rejected out of hand due to an international bias two years prior. This second analysis provided the following data of international athletes on the rosters: five of twenty-six team members, twelve of twenty-seven, nine of twenty-five (twice), nine of twenty-six, thirteen of thirty-two, nine of twenty-seven, and nine of twenty-three. This works out to international athletes averaging 36 percent of the rosters of our targeted colleges. I am not sure how my small data sample compares to the national average, but we felt that attempting to attract coaches who had a demonstrated focus on international athletes wouldn't work in Evan's favor.

Beginning of a sports journey at age two and half in August 2002. Credit: Karen Yeigh

First sports success as Fall 2007 champs. Credit: John Yeigh

Credit: Getty Images

Credit: Getty Images

Camaraderie and working as a team are two of the biggest benefits of youth sports. Credit: Getty Images

A pesky David versus scoring threat Goliath at age thirteen in 2013. Credit: Carolyn Kobosko

"Ordinary kids" in all sports and at all ages will benefit from focus, perseverance, and grit.

Credit: Getty Images

Credit: Getty Images

Credit: Getty Images

Credit: Getty Images

Credit: Karen Yeigh

Kid athletes can transition from short, thick, or awkward to lean and mean in just a couple growing seasons. Credit: Carolyn Kobosko

Incessant training led to a repeat selection on the Maryland state team and great abs in 2015. Credits: John Yeigh

Credit: Getty Images

Credit: Getty Images

Waiting on the bench is one of the single toughest challenge kids regularly face in youth sports. Credit: Getty Images

Continual training led to regular use of the weaker left foot. Credits: Carolyn Kobosko

County champs on the journey to Maryland state finals, 2017. Credit: John Yeigh

Battling in the high school playoffs versus one of many tough opponents in October 2017. Credit: *Capital Gazette*

Day 5,854 of a son's and father's journey on a 100°F-plus day in July 2018. Credit: John Yeigh

I also went back and checked the women's rosters for these same eight colleges, but that analysis yielded quite different results: three international players of twenty-eight total, two of twenty-seven, five of twenty-six, zero of twenty-nine, three of twenty-eight, five of twenty-nine, one of twenty-four, and five of thirty. As a percentage, international athletes comprised 11 percent of these women's rosters. Looked at together, the challenge of competing against international players for D1 roster slots is only one-third as problematic for girls as for boys. Yet this difference makes sense, since U.S. women's soccer is among the strongest internationally, while U.S. men's soccer is not. These analyses also show that the recruiting of international athletes is college, coach, and gender-specific.

The third challenge in gaining access D1 colleges occurs in active red-shirting. Just a couple of colleges seemed to redshirt one to two freshmen most years. While this might work for a student planning a five-year college experience, Evan sought a normal four-year academic experience. Redshirting turned out not to be a showstopper as we'd already eliminated any redshirt-happy college teams for their preference for international athletes.

Playing time was the fourth factor we analyzed [==]. Most college sports programs maintain and openly publish detailed individual player statistics, including minutes, innings, games, periods or halves played. While it takes time, trolling playing-time statistics can identify some of the trends surrounding how college coaches manage and utilize their athletes.

"There is no better coach than the bench." —Anson Dorrance, North Carolina women's soccer coach and twenty-two-time national champion

For example, a few college coaches rarely play freshmen and, to some extent, even sophomores. (Perhaps they're waiting for these players to further develop skills and physicality?) In contrast, major program men's basketball is uniquely dominated by freshman players due to the "one and done" system resulting from pro recruiting rules. Other coaches rely on just a few key junior and senior players, while the remainder of upperclassmen rarely see the field during games. These senior players receiving limited playing time seem to have effectively been relegated to be practice dummies. From a positive standpoint, this implies these D1 coaches may sustain an athlete's scholarship eligibility throughout their college career. But Evan had no desire to become a four-year practice dummy due to any coach's observable propensity to ignore freshmen or push aside seniors.

We also looked at playing time for some of Evan's contemporaries of similar ability. We had at least eight comparable examples of local athletes now on college teams who had played on his high school team or as an older member of his travel teams. One junior played zero minutes (D1), one junior was playing a reasonable amount of time each game (D1), one junior quit (D1), one sophomore played seven minutes (D1), and four freshmen played 273 (D3), 83 (D3), 54 (D1), and zero (D1) minutes. With the one exception, it was clear that most of Evan's contemporaries weren't getting much playing time early in their college careers.

This trend of limited freshmen play makes some sense, as freshmen are playing opponents who are three or more years older; I later discovered a few collegiate athletes, even in D3, are as old as twenty-five. This playing time information inferred that many athletes might have overshot their sports capabilities regarding their choice of colleges.

As hard as Evan and I worked the data—I call it "stalking" data—I have to caution that these kinds of analyses boil down to a snapshot view. You have some information, but not all of it. For instance, I later learned of one team where the freshmen received a fantastic amount of playing time—and it turned out that was due to six upperclassmen starters being suspended for alleged drug infractions.

Challenge number five we encountered was a strong bias for local and regional players [==], but it wasn't an issue that stood out right away. We actually discovered this bias late in the recruiting game, as one coach inadvertently articulated his strong bent for these players.

After being observed at a showcase tournament and receiving favorable feedback from the coach, Evan attended his ID camp. The college was a D3 engineering school, one we felt confident was a "soccer safety college." This college was in a distant state, and the camp's thirty players were by far the weakest of any camp Evan attended. The coach knew many of the campers, fondly chatting with them and calling them by name.

I believed just two campers had solid college-level ability. One was a striker from Virginia who had competed against Evan's travel team, attended four of the same ID camps, and was targeting the same engineering colleges. He'd even been Evan's roommate at two camps, making for several interesting coincidences. In my parentally biased opinion, Evan *crushed* it at this camp and was far and away the strongest midfielder. Likewise, his Virginia buddy was the strongest striker. The coach did personally single out and chat with the Virginia player and Evan. And then the Virginia player's parent advised me that his son had not gotten any serious traction with this coach.

I was oblivious to this coach's strong regional bias until his closing speech. In it, he highlighted that he has known several players for many years through youth play. He also stated that he especially enjoyed coaching locals on his ODP teams (which Evan's

Maryland ODP team had comfortably beaten), and then closed by asking all players to keep him apprised of progress through the local and regional high school playoffs. Why? Because he utilized those games as a primary scouting tool for his recruiting efforts. Ouch! Certainly, this coach had no intention of driving nine hours one way to watch Maryland or Virginia players in their state playoff games.

This speech put the nail in the coffin for this college, despite Evan liking the school's vibe. And I kicked myself, because I should have spotted this coach's bias at the outset. Sixty-five percent of his team's players had been sourced in-state, and all but one player hailed from in-state or the two adjacent states. This coach had recruited no player from the mid-Atlantic, midwestern, or southern states. In hindsight, this team had the least geographically diverse roster of any college under consideration.

In a similar but less obvious example of local favoritism, one D3 coach advised at the end of his ID camp that he intended to recruit just five players, none of which would be midfielders since he already had fourteen rostered. (No parent was brave enough to ask why he'd recruited midfielders to attend the paid camp since he had no intentions of rostering any.) He did eventually recruit one local midfielder to join his mostly locally sourced roster, and I couldn't complain at the choice as this midfielder was every bit as good as or better than Evan, and his recruiting video showed he had solid credentials. Yet, this was just another example where locals get the nod over kids from several states away.

As it turns out, college sports rosters are commonly comprised of mainly regional athletes due to the natural comfort, proximity, and recruiting ease. I wouldn't be surprised if this trend increases in the future due to the pandemic and any long-term impacts of socially distanced recruiting.

Another problem we came across, maybe surprisingly, was with coaches who over-recruit [==]. There were several versions of this issue.

One is a coach who carries a roster that's too big. Most college soccer teams roster twenty-five to thirty players (seven to nine new players per year), which enables eleven-versus-eleven practices and room to account for injuries, illnesses, and dropouts. Yet we found one college coach with a roster of forty-two. He openly acknowledged it was a problem. Two other target colleges had thirty-five or more players. It doesn't take a math genius to calculate that playing time at these colleges would be compromised.

Another example was found in a coach who recruited sixteen freshmen, where the recruits were advised up front that they would have to try out in the preseason for the eight available roster slots. No matter how you cut it, half the players who take the deal end up attending a college that won't provide the experience they're seeking.

At least the players knew what the jig was going in with that coach. I knew of another first-year college coach who over-recruited sixteen freshman (double the norm), but never told them how excessively large of an incoming class he had recruited.

These over-recruiting issues don't just happen in soccer. I knew of one college sailing team that had more than forty skippers rostered—a typical college sailing roster might have twelve to eighteen skippers who compete for six to twelve weekly starting slots, depending upon the number of events sailed. This college's sailing roster was clearly overloaded with athletes having to sit on the bench.

It would not be uncommon for the coaches of big programs to over-recruit in order to build in bench strength and, maybe, even weaken the available opposition just because they can. The roster depth is ridiculously overloaded in stronghold programs like Alabama or Clemson football, Connecticut women's basketball, and Maryland women's lacrosse. But college coaches who don't maintain a recruiting balance end up creating a four-year issue of playing time distribution and an underlying challenge for team harmony. Having truly exceptional athletes permanently parked on the bench does not foster a happy team environment, even if the team wins a national championship. Karen and I observed this situation with three extremely talented peers of our kids, in three different sports. These kids were on teams that won a championship but not thanks to these terrific athletes because they never really participated.

Something else to avoid is the college coach who's a bit wacky [==]. Discovering problematic personalities required some creative digging, since a Google search didn't give up the goods. With one of our initial target colleges, we learned the soccer coach was uniformly disliked by his players. This bit of information was gleaned from the parent of a former high school teammate of Evan's who attended that college but elected not to play soccer. Scratch that one off the list.

College visits with the team's players and overnight stays were perhaps the best way to get the scoop on a coach's demeanor. At one such visit to a college on his shortlist and where he was in active recruiting discussions with the coach, Evan received some surprising feedback on the coach from a totally unexpected source: the *admissions* staff.

After Evan presented his high school engineering portfolio to support the admissions process, the admissions counselor encouraged any and all questions. With much reservation, Evan cautiously advised that the coach's communications were inconsistent and confusing. The counselor surprisingly volunteered that the coach fostered successful teams but at times wasn't the best communicator. The counselor advised that players sometimes utilized other campus resources to "work around" the coach and suggested Evan should copy the athletic director on correspondence with the coach. We were stunned by the caution. After taking it in, and despite liking the college, we realized that signing on with a coach even the college admissions people acknowledge needs to be "worked around" was probably not the smartest plan.

In the future, the process of identifying both excellent and not-so-great coaches may become easier, as several ranking websites have recently come to life. These sites assess or review coaches in a manner similar to sites for teacher or restaurant assessments. Think of it as Yelp for coaches. These sites I'm familiar with include LRT-sports.com, Ratemycoaches.com, and Coachgrader.com.

One detraction from the usefulness of these sites is that thus far, there's no feedback on a large number of coaches, some coaches have feedback only on one of the sites, and, overall, the quantity of feedback is too small to be significant. And, just as with any ratings site, one disgruntled party can stuff the ballot box with lots of negative submissions, or a coach can have buddies fluff up the site with lots of positive comments. Still, this concept has merit and, hopefully, at least one of the sites will develop enough traction to be useful in the longer-term.

To further research coaches, again, Evan and I should have watched college soccer videos a year earlier in his college search. It's a simple "stalking" process that can provide a lot of understanding about prospective college teams and coaches, stuff you won't find on the glossy websites and brochures. For example, a couple of coaches who were yellers would have been identified early on [==] because some of their screaming came through loud and clear on the videos. We also, surprisingly, discovered some college programs that still played with a playground-like kick-and-chase approach. Such strategy has minimal possession or midfield buildup play [==]. One coach we viewed relied on strong athletes in the back and up top, much like some youth coaches in

Evan's U12 to U14 days. I'll say this loud and clear: A coach fostering a style of play inappropriate to the player should be a deal breaker. A drop back, pocket-passing quarterback just will not be a good fit for a triple-option running offense.

If I could, I'd go back with Evan and watch those game videos while we were working on his college selection list. Had we observed the coaches' demeanors and the teams' style of play first, we could have eliminated several colleges sooner and simplified the recruiting journey. That would have automatically saved us time, angst, and likely some funds invested in camps and traveling. The comforting takeaway, even in hindsight, is that the coaches who exhibited the strongest personal communication styles and positive ID camp interactions were the same coaches who displayed the best game mannerisms on video.

I'll repeat what I said in the previous chapter—watching the videos really helps. When it comes to working towards a beneficial college sports journey, this kind of homework can be invaluable.

Chapter 14

Finding the Sweet Spot for College Recruitment Success (U17-U18)

Evan experienced a growth period in his junior year of high school that physically transitioned him from a youth to a young man. His frame started to fill out, and he put on twenty pounds despite growing just an inch or so. He and his travel teammates also became starters on their high school team, in part a function of their new seniority as upperclassmen.

The high school team had a fantastic fall season, going 15–3–1 and making a deep playoff run to the Maryland State semifinals. Evan played the most playoff minutes of any non-defender, with just a few minutes on the sidelines due to a bloody leg. The team was disappointed to suffer the 2–0 playoff loss as they had beaten this same team during the regular season.

Travel sports just don't compare to the hype of having several hundred fans cheering and girlfriends holding up homemade banners with each player's name, picture, and a witty saying. Nor do high school sports have the cost or distance issues of travel-team sports, and they are much more inclusive in nature. However, the admission ticket to any decent high school team can take years of travel team play for most youth athletes.

We Started Early—Too Early

Evan and his travel teammates now began their college recruiting efforts in earnest. The team entered showcase tournaments and developed a team brochure highlighting each player's vital statistics, including grades, positions played, height, weight, and academic interests. The players also developed résumés, initiated contacts with coaches, and, in some cases, produced that highlight video and attended college ID camps. All the players were following the recommended "recruiting playbook," but most college coaches weren't taking a serious look at high school juniors (except to extoll the virtues of paying to attend their ID camps).

The Spring 2017 travel season of junior year, when the players were about to become rising seniors, was a prime recruiting period. The Fury team won Division 1 of the Region 1 league and was one game over 500 in Division 1 of the EDP league at U18. The Fury team never played at the U17 level, so its juniors played up one age group against seniors due to the adult organizational changes with the age-group makeup well discussed in Chapter 9.

The team encountered an even bigger challenge of having sufficient players for the Richmond, Jefferson, and Potomac Cup showcase tournaments. Tournament organizers schedule games for midday Friday, beginning with the U17 age group, thanks to a lack of fields and referees needed to complete all games on the weekends. In other words, athletes had to skip a school day for the Friday games of showcase tournaments, and naturally, that's a problem for students and their academics [==].

This is an unadvertised and ill-advised facet of the youth soccer (and many other sports) tournament systems, as academics and grades are critical for college admissions. While the showcase tournaments do provide an absence form a student can use to indicate the purpose of missing school is to meet college coaches, most school absences for travel-team events are considered unexcused. Missed homework and tests cannot be made up, resulting in lowered grades.

These regional tournament games held on Fridays are just the tip of the iceberg of missed schooling for elite athletes. High school athletes regularly have early dismissal for games, both home and away, though at least they're excused absences and work can be made up. Once, Evan's private school team traveled about six hours on a Friday to a Connecticut weekend tournament, and a couple of teachers penalized the grades of these players despite being a school-sanctioned activity. With random penalties like that, a high school GPA can easily tumble.

The biggest contributors to missed schooling are the travel-team tournaments *not* associated with high school sports. Some involve extensive car journeys and even airplane trips. For instance, our mid-Atlantic soccer tournaments included teams from as far away as Texas, Maine, and Florida. And though their families were obviously in a different league than the rest of us, I knew of two kids who regularly flew to sporting events on the family's private plane. In addition, when kids cross time zones to play sports, coaches and parents aren't going to send them directly onto the playing fields or courts because the athletes need extra time to recover from the travel before competing. All of which leads to missed schooling and the probability of lowered grades.

Evan's travel team participated in one tournament where just eight players mustered for Friday's game; most would not skip school. The coaches wisely had the team park the bus, playing a

4–2–1 formation with Evan assigned as the lone wolf up top. He was, in fact, tasked with being a one-man wrecking crew. His only assignment was to run around like a maniac and pressure the ball across the opposing team's midfield and defense.

It worked! Evan eventually ran out of gas, but with one fresh teammate arriving with ten minutes remaining and scoring in the last minute, Fury eked out a stunning 1–0 win.

The players still talk about this game years later. It's is probably my favorite game of all time, despite Evan's sole contribution being that he ran around non-stop for two-thirds of the game. He harassed the opponents to exasperation, while the defense made sure the opponents never scored. Even more remarkable, all nine teammates were "sick with colds" that Friday morning.

Camped Out

As noted previously, Evan attended lots of college ID camps between his freshman and junior years. We did this because every advisor we came across—coaches, the web, books, recruiters—recommended that athletes initiate recruiting as early as possible. Karen and I also discovered these camps provided a way to get a somewhat disinterested kid to check out lots of colleges.

Evan agreed to participate in the camps to help satisfy his non-stop demand for more soccer. He visited twenty-two target colleges, fourteen for soccer camps, four for engineering camps, and nine for separate coach or campus visits (see Appendix I). He also visited a few colleges multiple times. Through it all, we made sure he followed NCAA recruiting rules in initiating communications with any D1 coaches. D1 coaches in all sports have restrictions on their recruiting communications and athlete interactions which can be found on NCAA.org.

In the end, these early camps and networking visits with college coaches did almost nothing for recruiting. Evan participated in a couple of D1 camps late in his junior year where he played especially well and received some notice. One coach advised him, "My assessment from camp was only the start of our conversation, and I am looking forward to seeing you play more this summer and next fall." Another coach emailed, "I also was impressed with how comfortable you were on the ball. You are still young, and I will be excited to see how you continue to grow and develop physically. Please stay in touch with our coaching staff regarding your soccer schedule." In other words, "You're too early, kid!"

It's also important to note that for every positive college coach connection highlighted in Appendix III, there is an equivalent number of college coaches Evan never heard from. At one D1 camp, Evan was awarded "Camper of the Week," yet the coach never followed up. Evan wasn't alone. His peers in a variety of sports, even some with exceptional credentials and accolades, reported minimal success in their communications with coaches.

In fairness to the coaches, they receive multitudes of daily "recruit me" emails. The statistics confirm that, at best, one in twenty athletes might be a match for any particular program. In the individual discussions and at the camps, several coaches openly acknowledged being deluged with emails and voluntarily apologized for any missed communications.

Evan attended one ID camp in late April of his junior year where the coach advised that he was looking to finalize the last couple of slots for his freshmen recruiting class for the *current year's* September season four months hence. Wait, did we hear that correctly? Several parents were so stunned they asked the coach to repeat his statement, which he did. By April of their senior year, students will have long since submitted their applications, received admissions decisions, and paid their deposit to the college of choice. These seniors are well past their sell-by date for sports recruiting.

We followed all the advisors' playbooks to start recruiting activities super early, only to find out they were basically wrong. The only advantage of starting the recruiting journey so early on was that Evan got to practice his communication skills with coaches. Efforts late in the athlete's junior and early senior years of high school hit the sweet spot although girls tend to be recruited somewhat earlier. However, any college coach expecting athletes to wait until April of their senior year for a final roster decision will lose all the better students, because all athletes with reasonable academic options will be committed by then. Parents will make sure a college admission is cemented by the close of senior year regardless the pursuit of sports.

Chapter 15

Glossy Brochures and What "Lies" Within

"Be seen by 89.99 college coaches."

"We've had campers commit to D1 colleges."

"Play in front of D1, D2, D3, and DWhatever coaches."

"Supercallafragilistic Camp has two zillion players from all 53 states."

Smoke and Mirrors

Brochures advertising college sports camps are certainly enticing, and Evan and I were sucked in. Maybe the brochures were technically correct, but collegiate sports camps and combines have plenty of things to worry about that aren't openly advertised or readily apparent to naïve parents [==]. These sales pitches with their extended (false?) promises transcend all youth sports. For example:

- Of the 89.99 coaches, none may represent a college with the specific academic program in which the athlete is interested.

- Of the 89.99 coaches attending, it's a sure bet more than a few are the assistant to the assistant coach or just a former player, in other words, a person who has no real recruiting authority.
- Assistant coaches are often the one who shows up at the generic, large attendance camps because they are paid by the camp director to attend, and/or they receive a few days of paid hotel and vacation time.
- Campers advertised as D1 players were committed to their D1 colleges long before attending the advertised camp.
- High school seniors are segregated. They receive more serious assessments/attention, while underclassmen may be assigned to play on remote fields a couple of towns away.
- Athletes with strong pedigrees—four-star recruit, highest level academy play, or rostered on a top-ranked travel team—will be assigned to preselected camp teams or to the final all-star team for extra looks. Ordinary kids may not have a realistic chance to be noticed before the camp starts.
- The camp may have an attendance of 500 campers per field—good luck getting playing time.
- The camp or combine is based exclusively on short-sided or training-type games and drills due to the excessive number of campers squeezed on each field or court. Campers may be lucky to play one full-sided game.
- 1.9999 of the two zillion campers are midfielders, setters, wide receivers, outfielders, or point guards—*get in line.*
- Players may have to shift playing positions to obtain any meaningful time on the field because not enough teammates on their assigned camp team will be willing or able to play tough or less glamorous defensive positions.
- The team to which your player is assigned may be total crap. Weak players make your player look horrible, rather

than highlighting their abilities. Bad teams and the lowest common denominator in player abilities can be a never-ending constant of camps regardless the sport.

- College coaches may continue to promote their ID camps after their current year commitments are completed, almost surely based on the long-shot hope of a superstar making an appearance. (Evan still receives invites as a rising senior in college.)
- Directors of large camps may have no job other than running those camps. In addition, camps are a significant supplemental income generator for sponsoring coaches, organizers, field owners, and even the town's hospitality industry.

Once we figured out the truth behind the brochure stories, Evan stopped attending any large, generic sports camp. I felt, and Evan agreed, that these camps did not provide training worthy of the money invested, nor any potential to be magically discovered out of the morass of campers. We met with one college coach who stunned us by admitting that he had "never identified a single recruit from a large sports camp." Most coaches that we encountered honestly advised us that their rostered players were identified primarily through their own ID sports camps or visibility at a showcase tournament. Ordinary players clearly need to develop direct rapport and a connection with the coach to have any hopes of being identified and recruited.

Do You Need a Closer to Seal the Win?

While we bought into the camp brochure hype for too long, we didn't make the same mistake of utilizing a barrage of recruiting services to help make connections with college coaches. It's not that we didn't know they existed. Organizations that pinged Evan or we checked out included Captain U, BeRecruited, Scouting Zone, AthleticScholarships, NCSAsports, CollegeCoaches, Sports Contact USA, and RecruitLook. (Note: The names of these companies that help with recruiting are constantly evolving and could be different today.)

There are plenty more. They all have excellent and alluring websites and offer sound recruiting advice. Most assist athletes in a variety of different sports, just a few were soccer-focused recruiters, and some appeared to maintain networks of regional coaches or colleges. The recruiting process is a complex and imperfect game, so it's really no wonder so many companies have sprouted up to help manage the process.

One reason we didn't use a recruiting service was because Evan's desire for a mid-sized engineering college in the eastern U.S. had already narrowed his list to about thirty colleges. The recruiting agencies' algorithm-based recommendations mainly proposed smaller (safety) colleges that did not have engineering programs. Another reason was that coaches had universally indicated they preferred communicating directly with the athlete (see Appendix III) rather than recruiting via an intermediary.

Perhaps most importantly, we declined to use a recruiting agency because I felt we could manage this process without the additional support or cost. Why? For one thing, Evan's résumé was more robust than that generated by any recruiter's automated service. And despite sending his résumé directly to coaches, some still asked for his GPA or travel-team details. This information was listed on his résumé *and* entered on the coach's recruiting website. The only conclusion to draw is that coaches do not review résumés, including those of athletes with whom they are directly involved in recruiting dialogue.

Recruiter websites did offer the potential advantage of being readily searchable by coaches, but figuring out which recruiter(s) might be best for any particular kid or targeted college creates even more challenges. We also knew that college coaches are bombarded with inquiries from potential recruits, most more than they need. So, why would a coach seek more recruits from a middleman website?

These professional secondary party recruiters undoubtedly help some kids keep their recruiting process moving along or succeed in making needed connections, otherwise they wouldn't be in business. It's not hard to find positive results confirmed by client testimonials (although for soccer, most seem to be from girls rather than boys). One recruiter listed only a single boys' soccer testimonial from 2012, so either their 2017 website was outdated, or the company didn't have much success in this sport with boys over the past five years. Just recently, I found a 2006 testimonial featured on a 2021 website.

College Recruiting Is No Layup

While professional help is not mandatory, the recruiting process, regardless of sport or gender, does require a significant amount of parental support. This process is, in essence, akin to developing and implementing a complete business marketing plan.

I determined that college sports recruiting is a complex ten-step process and requires constant follow-up over an eighteen-month period beginning late in the athlete's sophomore year (maybe earlier for girls) and continuing through the early portion of their senior year. These ten steps include:

1. Begin initial market research, investigating colleges for appropriate fit (size, academics, vibe, and sports appropriateness).
2. Assess the competition (determine how one's sports abilities fit a particular college).

3. Develop a marketing and communication strategy aimed at potential coaches.
4. Develop an eighteen-month recruiting process timeline, ensuring all communications and college visits are completed prior to the athlete's senior year.
5. Create an advertising and product-differentiation plan that includes a résumé, cover email, and video highlighting sports accomplishments.
6. Implement the initial marketing communications strategy, communicating with targeted coaches and filling out their online questionnaires.
7. Implement selected product placement, with the athlete attending key ID camps or showcase tournaments.
8. Reassess and narrow the marketing strategy on a regular basis (identifying the final target colleges based on traction with the coaches per Appendix III).
9. Determine budgets in conjunction, assessing what colleges can offer financially and what the family can afford.
10. Follow through with final implementation of the revised marketing strategy to include final communications with coaches and admissions, taking part in overnight visits, completing SAT/ACT tests, improving grades, etc.

The pundit advice is that athletes should undertake all these project management and marketing activities by themselves—what a total bunch of bull. I don't know of one high school student who can manage these kinds of recruiting activities without the help of their parents. We assisted with most of Evan's activities except the direct email, phone, and meeting communications with the coaches. We also proofread his later, more serious email communications before he hit the send key. *All* parents we talked to assisted their athletes during the recruiting process in a similar manner.

College recruiting is a long and arduous journey for any athlete. The industrial sports complex offers plenty of organizational support for the athletes at a cost, but the camps, coaches, organizers, and recruiters too often oversell the likely outcomes. As Evan, his teammates, and peers in other sports progressed in their recruiting journeys, they were constantly solicited to participate in various paid camps, tournaments, lectures, and other recruiting activities. Despite the opportunities, we found it increasingly difficult for Evan to benefit in proportion to the time commitment and cost, particularly with the many camps that didn't begin to approach collegiate playing levels [==]. In the end, once the list of potential colleges has been whittled down to something manageable, elite athletes should cut to the chase and concentrate on those colleges where the fit or connection stands out.

Chapter 16

Closing Out the Journey Toward College (U18-U19)

Emails, showcase tournaments, camps, more emails, website searching, virtual college tours, zillions of camp invites, "stalking" college coaches, deferred coach interest, more camps, in-person college tours, video editing, coach meetings, zillions of application invites, essays, more emails, coaches not replying, early decisions, revised essays, coach limited interest, early action decisions, phone discussions, admissions meetings, scholarship applications, and overnights. Wash, rinse, repeat.

What does all this get a high school athlete? Burnout.

Then comes the realization that athletes must focus on finding the best college atmosphere and academic situation. Many highly recruitable athletes give up on their dream of playing college sports, not because of ability but because of recruiting hurdles. The recruiting journey for talented but ordinary athletes is incredibly difficult. Of course, the problems aren't so pronounced when it comes to playing for smaller or less competitive college programs, but these institutions may not offer the ideal curricula, academic challenges, or avenues to a career. For example, two coaches from solid but smaller local colleges advised the travel-team coach that they'd willingly accept any of the team's starters onto their roster.

Free Agency Until Signing

Evan locked in and committed to a D3 engineering college with solid academics and job placement success before his high school senior year began. He respected the coach, and it appeared he'd be able to contribute to the soccer program and not just become a four-year practice dummy. The college offered some financial support based on academic merit, which confirmed that good grades pay as much as exceptional athletic abilities. Most of Evan's cohorts moving on to college play in a variety of sports and levels (D1, D2, and D3) had committed to their college choice by February of their senior years.

One teammate had to scramble late in his senior year as his committed college hadn't followed through with its promised financial support. Who knew that colleges or their coaches might renege on agreed terms [==]? This athlete was not only a talented player but also very strong academically. He and his family were able to gain admission to an alternative college and sports program, but it took a nearly full-time effort over the months leading up to the April admissions commitment period to secure the slot.

This example demonstrates that even though a student-athlete may be well placed, it's important to try to maintain some college optionality throughout the recruiting journey. Finances are not the only reason to maintain options. Injuries, a change in academic interest, family issues, and financial disruptions can change the course for the student. So, too, can changes in academic programs, coaching staff, team configurations, probation periods, pandemic shutdowns, the crazy "Varsity Blues" scandal, and even team dissolution can quickly undo what a family had thought was a clear path forward [==].

For example, a coach can recruit a number of five-star players which seriously diminishes long-term playing prospects for even the most highly talented. Who would have believed that Kyler Murray (Heisman Trophy winner), Jalen Hurts (prior NCAA national champion), and Joe Burrow (Heisman Trophy winner) all had to transfer colleges just to get playing time? Recently, a number of prominent D1 colleges eliminated a variety of varsity sports. One was the University of Cincinnati, which terminated its men's D1 soccer program after nearly fifty years. Evan was actively recruited at one D1 college where he was among just a handful of players invited to private camp sessions with the coach and team. This promising opportunity disappeared in an instant when the coach moved on to the pros and the new coach jettisoned the shortlist of previously targeted players. Although Evan had no backup plan, in hindsight, I feel we should have maintained more college options.

Runners-Up

With the stress of recruiting behind him, Evan was able to focus on and enjoy his senior year. Others continued wading through the recruiting quagmire. For all, it turned out to be quite a year. The Severna Park high school team had fifteen seniors who had played on Evan's Fury travel team at one time or another. The players knew each other well and had developed great camaraderie. Five teammates would go on to play in college, and at least another three had college offers. The team was undefeated through the regular season at 14–0–1, won the county championship, and was ranked number one in Maryland and as high as twelfth nationally at one point. It wasn't an easy road as three games were won in overtime, including two against the exceptionally tough archrival Meade High School.

In playoffs, Evan's team dispatched one weaker team and then faced three of Maryland's toughest opponents in a row—Meade, Leonardtown, and Bowie. These highly ranked opponents had each won fourteen or more games. The Meade game resulted in a third overtime battle with this team, but this time there would be no golden-goal winner—the game would be decided on penalty kicks. Severna Park fell behind on its kicks at one point, but won on the sixth penalty kick to squeak by the Meade team for the third time that season.

Severna Park (18–0–1) moved on to meet Bethesda (13–3–3) in the Maryland state championship game. Bethesda was the underdog, but it, likewise, had beaten three highly ranked teams on its way to the finals. Several thousand fans awaited a tough and exciting game.

Sports can be cruel. Severna Park had five good shots on goal without scoring, but then Bethesda's lone shot hit the back of the net with just ninety ticks remaining on the clock. Bethesda played well and was the fairy tale team of destiny. Despite the loss, Severna's coach received numerous accolades, including county Coach of the Year honors. The team's success was also largely a result of the long-standing travel team, and Coaches Kenny and K deserve much credit for the high school team's achievements.

While greatly disappointed by the final game's outcome, Evan was truly happy about his performances in the playoff run. He had been the single non-defender who played nearly every minute throughout that run, relegated to the sideline for only a couple of brief minutes when he drew an intentional yellow-card infraction (he took one for the team with a last-ditch foul from behind as he covered for one of his fullbacks who had been beaten). After the semifinals, the coach even hugged and commended Evan for having his "best game ever." Evan the "hop-on" had become the team's stalwart defensive midfielder during his final two seasons.

Though the team didn't walk away with the championship, the tremendously successful season had been a joy to watch. The team conceded a miserly 10 goals over 20 games that included 11 shutouts. That success was due to the four excellent defensive backs, two strong keepers, and the defensive midfielders, including primary holding midfielder Evan. While the low opponent scoring might imply a focus on a parking-the-bus approach, the team also scored a stellar 61 goals.

Standing with the Friends You Make

Three weeks after Evan's high school journey concluded, the U19 travel team was back in action with a showcase tournament. It was a bittersweet experience for me. This senior year travel season would be my last opportunity to enjoy watching all these players who had grown up together. Seven had been together continuously for seven years on the travel team, as well as Evan's three years on the high school team. I would miss that special camaraderie I had developed with their parents through rain, sleet, gloom of night, and three-hour drives. I shared more than half of Evan's 719 games with these same parents.

Throughout the journey, I was a "stander" at the games. Most parents and guests on the sidelines were sitters, utilizing those popular portable folding chairs designed for sports spectators. "Deluxe" chairs were a standard, outfitted with a sun canopy, footrest, headrest, padded seat, cup holder, and other features. These were supplemented with blankets in the winter, play tents and toys for the younger kids, sunscreen, hats and gloves, wheeled coolers, snack bags, and even battery-powered fans. A clandestine adult beverage might have been surreptitiously consumed during an evening game or two. I have camped for a week with less gear than some parents lugged in for a single game.

I found standing provided the most unobstructed view of the games. Even for games in stadiums, I stood at the top of the stands. I stationed myself toward the defensive end of the field, since this was where Evan was positioned most of the time.

During my sideline excursions, I enjoyed the company of the rec-league, travel team, and high school parents throughout the years, even the clique parents. I still maintain friendly connections with a few of the U7 to U10-era coaches and parents more than a decade later. I suspect the favorable connections with all the parents reflected the positive team approach of all the players. During the U9 to U10 years, we did have among our ranks a couple of psycho parents who were all and only about their child, and they let that be known at every opportunity. A couple of these "Billy, you are *best* player!" or "Billy, *shoot,* don't pass!" parents existed in the earliest years but faded away as competitive travel sports took hold.

> "Teamwork is what makes common people capable of uncommon results." —Pat Summitt, Tennessee women's basketball coach and eight-time national champion

To their credit, neither the travel team nor high school coaches ever tolerated selfish players, nor did the teams ever have that "special" superstar. These players lived and died as a team, and the positive playing style resulted in good parental harmony. Players had different skill sets, physical abilities, and energy. Individual performances on any given day were highly variable as might be expected with a set of hormonal teenagers, but the parents were always positive about the team.

Over the years, my favorite fellow bystanders were Mike, Bruce, and Sloan. Our four sons were all positioned toward the defensive end of the pitch. These three fathers had a good sense for the game and would acknowledge when our team was getting slaughtered by a more skilled opponent; they were without pretense and never felt the need to sugarcoat the games or performances.

All the team's moms were balanced and relentlessly positive, the perfect sideline parents. One mom was brutally tough about her own son's play, but otherwise positive. Perhaps the best cheerleading parent was Tim, who never uttered so much as an under-breath groan about any player who'd had a bad play.

While most parents were fully supportive, there are always a few who didn't always pull their weight when it came to volunteer support or recognition of those who did contribute. Twice, I took it upon myself to get thank-you cards for the travel-team coaches and team manager for end-of-season parties (keeping in mind they were unpaid volunteers). Getting all the signatures was like pulling teeth. I get that the parents of players not receiving ideal playing time might be hesitant to acknowledge or reward the coaches, but how about at least signing the team manager's card? My kid was among those who sometimes had more than his share of bench time, but some acknowledgment or appreciation for the coaches committing lots of their free time was certainly the right thing to do.

These same parents freely signed cards and chipped in each year for the paid high school coaches. After my second time trying to collect card signatures for our volunteer coaches, I simply forged a couple of unreadable signatures, contributed extra money, and vowed to forevermore go our own way with recognition. I was proud that Evan had developed the good habit of thanking the coaches after practices and games. Even better, Evan, with the help of his girlfriend, babysat the coach's child while we took the long-term coach and his wife out for a farewell dinner.

Along this journey, I loved watching both the travel and high-school teams play, just as I enjoyed watching my daughter's teams in their water-based sports. I was never bothered by pouring rain, blistering heat, or frigid cold. I liked *everything* about watching youth sports, even if the game or my kid's play wasn't so special. Each competition was part of development and growth.

I'm unsure if my strong interest in watching my kids resulted from my parents never attending my sports activities or just a natural shift wrought by today's generation of helicopter parents. The expectation for parents today is that they should watch every moment of their kids' activities and be totally involved. I grew up in a different era, and parents didn't watch a lot of their kids play sports; my parents were fine about picking me up, but they never watched.

Short-Sided Play

The spring of Evan's senior year in high school was supposed to be the conquered ending to the travel-team journey, a youth-sports victory lap into the sunset. I was reveling in this final year of my son's play when I arrived to watch one game at a big tournament just as the game started. I was stunned to see midfielder Evan as the lone center-back of a three-back line of defenders. *What were the coaches thinking*?

As the starting whistle blew, I started counting off players with my fingers—I didn't have to go to my toes to include the goalkeeper. The team was set up in a 3-3-1 formation, rather than the usual 4-4-2, for an eight-versus-eleven play. Evan's team played very well but lost a close game, without a doubt the result of being three players short. The rest of the tournament delivered more of the same.

In the next tournament two weeks later, midfielder Evan was again playing center back. The team played three more shorthanded games, all within forty-eight hours. Opponents showed up with a roster of sixteen to eighteen players, which gave them up to seven substitutes, so even weaker opponents prevailed as their roster depth helped grind out wins.

Three days later, Coach Kenny sensibly shut down the team after nearly ten successful years; it had succumbed to a terminal case of senioritis. This unforeseen shutdown was problematic for the college-committed players who needed to maintain training over the next five months until their college preseasons started. Like most parents, we had no backup plan in place.

The Hail-Mary Pass

Evan and I immediately approached the coach of a team one age group down (U18) from where Evan and his team had been playing because of the age group issues discussed earlier. This team was called Juventus and was ranked fifteenth in the country, much higher than Fury. The coach called me back within an hour, and I was prepped to grovel, beg, plead, cajole, or financially entice (yes, I had my wallet preset on "bribe") him to take on Evan, even if only for practice sessions.

Luck was on our side. Juventus ("Juve" as they were known) had encountered several injuries and its own case of senioritis. In that short hour before he called back, Coach Pat had performed a quick scouting review of Evan with other coaches he knew. Based on their positive feedback, he added Evan to his team's roster without a tryout, a first for us, and he wanted Evan rostered in time for a Saturday game just forty hours hence.

Evan and I had to speed through the bureaucratic rostering procedures, something we hadn't had to do in several years. The most difficult step was obtaining an authorized release from the old team, which no longer existed and had no remaining officials. The old Fury team manager handled this graciously and expeditiously, even though the team's demise meant he no longer had any true authority. Evan was officially rostered by midday Friday and playing in a game Saturday morning.

We had worried the death of Fury might create a training problem, but its ending turned out to be a blessing for Evan. He played on Juventus without missing a beat. Juve's roster was comprised mostly of juniors still seeking college commitments, its few seniors were college commits, and unlike Fury, Juve had already shed those kids checking out of youth sports.

The Juventus switch helped reinvigorate Evan's growth as a player. He encountered an excellent new coach, new teammates, diverse playing styles, revised training regimes, fresh banter, and even a new position. With injuries to several defensive players, Evan moved into the fullback position, where he could play with gusto, as there were no longer concerns about impending tryouts or political baggage. Evan needed Juve, and Juve needed him equally. Coach Pat, to his credit, treated all the players equally, and these final few months turned out to be a refreshing change.

In his final youth-sports year, Evan relished the amazing run he was having. In a way, the successful high school season was a culmination of the sixteen-year journey for all the teammates. By then, Evan was happily committed to an excellent engineering college that had a solid soccer program, and glad to have the stressful recruiting process behind him. He especially enjoyed the refreshing playing experiences with Juventus. He was back to playing sports merely for the passion and joy of it, just as he had as a peewee player. And that's what kids' sport journeys should always be about.

Chapter 17

Your Kid May Be Special—but They're Not Getting a D1 Scholarship

U.S. youth-sports participation in general, and soccer in particular, is big, *very* big. Athletic scholarship numbers, though, are small, *very* small. Youth sport organizers don't always acknowledge just how dire is the imbalance between the two—but this Barcalounger analysis can provide some insight.

In the 2006 official FIFA (Federation International Football Association or governing organization) "big count," the U.S. was at or near the top in soccer participation. FIFA indicated total participation in the U.S. was twenty-five million (second in the world to China's twenty-six million). In youth soccer, the U.S. was first in registered participation with four million kids with far more boys than girls.

According to a more recent 2014 Sports and Fitness Industry Association (SFIA) study, the total number of youth soccer players was nearly eight million, second to basketball's nearly ten million participants. While multiple studies indicate both youth sports and youth soccer participation has leveled out or declined over the last few years, youth soccer is still amazingly healthy. Its huge numbers deliver fantastic playing opportunities, but the numbers also result in daunting competition to get noticed by college coaches.

Getting Shut Out

In 2017, men's college soccer had 205 D1 programs. With average rosters of about twenty-eight players, total D1 athletes fall between 5,500 and 6,000. This translates to a recruiting class size of about 1,500 each year.

I've previously explained that many D1 roster slots are filled by international players. My very limited analysis indicates that, in recent years, they may take as much as 36 percent of the available slots. A broader estimate is available on Coach Up's excellent website, Scholarshipstats.com, which analyzes recruiting data for most major college sports. This website provides a more conservative estimate for internationals D1 participation at 16 percent. So, excluding even that conservative 16 percent for international players leaves only about 1,250 D1 roster slots per year remaining for North American kids.

About 450,000 boys play U.S. high school soccer, this number quoted by many sources including NCAA.org, which provides participation data for most collegiate sports. Perhaps 112,500 high school seniors aspire to fill the 1,250 D1 freshman roster slots. This implies a 1 percent success rate for high school players, again quoted by organizations including the NCAA.

Wrong! The math is correct, but the inference of where these D1 recruits are sourced is not. U.S. Soccer's Development Academies had seventy-four U18/U19 boy's teams comprised of players who largely did *not* participate in high school play. Assuming an average roster size of twenty-two players, the Development Academies have perhaps 1,600 athletes in the college freshman recruiting age range. Even if half of those are ineligible (not seniors, not academically qualified, going pro), the Development Academies still produce a pool of perhaps 800 highly qualified players available for the 1,250 D1 roster slots each year.

Many D1 roster slots are filled by players from the Development Academy (or the latest structural incarnation). I followed this trend for 2018 high school graduates on Topdrawersoccer.com, which I found to be the best at reporting soccer commitments in addition to other youth news and rankings. We also checked out Maxpreps.com, which reports recruiting information for about twenty different boys' and girls' sports. Other high school team rankings, elite recruiting rankings (number of stars), and recruiting information websites include, 247Sports.com (a sister of MaxPreps.com), Rivals.com, and ESPN.com.

This leaves perhaps four hundred to six hundred D1 roster slots remaining to be filled by elite, non-Development Academy travel and high school players. By this math, the likelihood of obtaining a D1 roster slot declines to something less than half of 1 percent or below one in two hundred for ordinary U.S. high school players (without even considering Canadian players who often come south).

The industry estimate is that about eight million U.S. kids play soccer. Assuming sixty percent are boys, that yields 4.8 million boys spread across the twelve-year youth-sports time spectrum. This suggests peak participation is on the order of 450,000 in the early age brackets. Extrapolated, the odds of any field full of peewees making it to D1 soccer are no higher than a paltry one in 350. In fact, the odds even for high school athletes being accepted to *any* collegiate program, let alone a D1 program, are not at all great (see the following table taken from scholarshipstats.com).

Collegiate Sport	Odds of Playing at College	Odds of Playing D1
MEN'S		
Football	1 in 11	1 in 69
Baseball	1 in 9	1 in 50
Basketball	1 in 18	1 in 105
Soccer	1 in 14	1 in 99
Ice Hockey	1 in 24	1 in 52
WOMEN's		
Volleyball	1 in 18	1 in 91
Softball	1 in 12	1 in 64
Basketball	1 in 15	1 in 83
Soccer	1 in 11	1 in 46
Ice Hockey	1 in 9	1 in 28

Show Me the Money

These are the tough odds of a youth player obtaining a D1 roster spot. The odds of receiving a full D1 athletic scholarship are far, far worse. D1 men's soccer teams are allowed 9.9 scholarships for their average roster of twenty-eight players. That equates to about a 35 percent scholarship rate per D1 athlete or two-and-a-half scholarships per academic year. A few exceptional athletes may receive a full athletic scholarship, leaving even less money for mere mortal recruits.

Many D1 soccer programs do not have full athletic scholarship funding, something not openly advertised. We found this out during a D1 college visit where we were told the college had absolutely no (yes, zero!) soccer scholarship funding. Nor did many of their competing colleges in the same league. Ivy League colleges (D1) do not fund athletic scholarships. With 205 D1 colleges and, at best, two-and-half funded scholarships per year for men's soccer teams, fewer than four hundred D1 full soccer scholarships are available each year. In fact, the NCAA advises that only about 2 percent of high school athletes across all sports receive some athletic scholarship funding.

Bottom line, the likelihood of even a partial D1 athletic soccer scholarship is dismal for high school players [==]. The good news is that 33,000-plus collegiate playing opportunities exist in:

- NCAA D2 (~ 6,000)
- NCAA D3 (~ 12,000)
- NAIA (~ 6,000)
- NJCAA (junior colleges ~ 5,000)
- Other colleges (maybe 5,000)

These opportunities expand the potential for high school soccer players to play somewhere in college to something like 5 or 6 percent. In addition, the following soccer scholarships can be offered:

- D2 – 9
- D3 – 0
- NAIA – 12
- NJCAA – 18
- Other colleges – varies

These non-D1 colleges significantly increase the potential collegiate scholarships, but total athletic scholarship opportunities are still small since the biggest collegiate group, NCAA D3, does not offer athletic scholarships.

The missing piece of the puzzle exists in merit (academic) scholarships. These are far more plentiful and often larger than athletic scholarships. For example, 80 percent of all D3 athletes received some level of academic scholarship support, according to the NCAA, and this averaged $17,000 in 2017. This implies that, if given the choice between improved grades and improved athletic skills, mathletes win every time.

Title IX Seems to Work

Collegiate soccer scholarship opportunities for girl high school athletes are higher than for boys.

- Girls have about two-thirds the total players compared to boys.
- Girls have 333 D1 colleges to select from versus 205 D1 colleges for boys.
- D1 colleges can offer women 14 scholarships versus 9.9 for men.
- International players make up 6 percent of players on women's college teams versus 16 percent (or much higher by my research) for men's teams.
- Girls had sixty-nine Development Academy U18/19 teams (these started up in 2017) versus the well-established seventy-four boys' teams (these have been around since 2007).

The increased scholarship advantage for girls is largely due to the Title IX requirement to offset the sixty-five to eighty-five men's football scholarships. Solid girl high school soccer athletes are clearly more in demand than boys.

The math might imply that high school girls' opportunities for D1 soccer are about double compared to boys. My observations suggest there's a higher demand than the math might indicate. Girls are recruited one to two years earlier than boys, a conclusion drawn from Topdrawersoccer.com. In an extreme example, the University of North Carolina committed to an eleven-year-old girl who would not be playing for them for *seven years* (one year later, the girl reneged on the UNC commitment and turned pro). Recruitment at such an age would *never* happen for a boy.

I discovered three other pieces of evidence that girls are in higher demand. First, all the professional recruiting services promote testimonials mostly from girls, with few from boys; the ratio I saw was about ten to one. Second, much advice about successful soccer recruiting posted on the web relates to girls, even when gender isn't specified in the search. Finally, we bought the only three college soccer recruiting guidebooks I could find at the time: *Get Recruited to Play Women's College Soccer*, *Pigtails to Preseason,* and *A Parent's Guide to College Soccer Recruiting*. Although the title of the third book is generic, the content relates to successful recruiting for the author's four daughters. In other words, lots of websites and books highlight the successful college recruiting processes for girls, but the recruiting situation is far tougher for their male counterparts.

While sports scholarship odds are small, athletes do gain an admissions acceptance advantage at elite colleges. College admission requirements (grades, testing scores, essays, etc.) are generally lower when an athlete is on the coach's recruitment list. The admission preference for athletes is well known and perhaps best documented in a 2019 article in *The Atlantic* that reported, "90 percent of recruited athletes gain admission to Harvard, versus about 6 percent of applicants overall." For well-off families, the admission advantages may be more important than the financial benefits of an athletic scholarship. Still, before arriving at a fork in the road in their college recruiting journey, athletes and their parents should be aware that the inherent math for D1 athletic scholarships is fundamentally abysmal.

Epilogue

Uniforms, otherwise known as the "soccer kit," were purchased in two versions: light and dark or home and away. Evan's teams were adorned in white and red, white and blue, white and black, and white and green. Evan, fortunately, was never cloaked in any of horrible bright orange, fuchsia, or chartreuse; the goalkeepers definitely donned some dazzling neon hues perhaps to scare off attacking strikers.

New uniforms were not required every year, as the kids could often wear them for two seasons in the early, low-growth years. (What sports parent *doesn't* order a kid's uniform with room to grow in the hopes of saving a few bucks next season?) This resulted in the phenomenon of having a kid in a droopy, oversized jersey every other year in the team picture.

Adidas is a global leader for soccer apparel, so I was not surprised that half of the uniforms included the three stripes and Climalite logos. We also live near Under Armour's Baltimore home, and that company sponsors many local teams. Here's how the uniform brand tally figured for Evan's twelve years in youth soccer:

1. Adidas – seven
2. Under Armour – three
3. Beefy Tee – two
4. No brand name – two
5. Nike – zero

These are the companies that supplied the team uniform, or rather the company from which we were held hostage for purchasing the official uniform decreed by the various team organizations. And, yes, Nike was a big fat zero.

Since Nike is the U.S. sports apparel leader, I was surprised Evan's uniforms never once included the swoosh logo, although he did own some swoosh-adorned cold weather compression shirts. Despite this, I have no concern for Nike's bottom line or its co-founder and chairman emeritus, Phil Knight, as Nike has been the "official" cleat supplier to Evan's feet since age ten.

He has recently been wearing the most expensive Nike Mercurial cleats, which are incredibly light. For these few ounces of extruded plastic, we enjoy the privilege of paying Mr. Knight nearly $300. The best part is that Nike doesn't even charge extra for that festering, road kill stink that becomes permanently and indelibly melded into the plastic. Even storing the boots in a vat of Febreze doesn't purge the embedded stink. The only consolation is that these cleats last a year at most, which provides the athletes with a recurring opportunity to imbue a new pair with the latest *Eau de Teenage Foot Funk*.

Despite our smelly cleat challenges, I'm told that nothing compares to the stench of hockey gear stuffed into their large carry bags. Our family can likewise attest to the reek of bundles of wet sailing gear, especially after competitions held on brackish waters. Any dedicated sports family would benefit from having a house with a separate laundry, entranceway, closet, or garage to accommodate the requisite daily gear-drying ritual.

Time and Money, Money and Time

Speaking of feet, friends regularly ask Karen and me if the journey was worth it. Some just can't get their heads wrapped around the commitment needed for travel sports. I voted with my feet hundreds of times, standing by the sidelines to watch games. Both friends and family have lamented our absence at various events and celebrations over the years that we missed due to youth sports—"Sorry, Evan's got a game." Travel sports mandated a ten-year family time-out from large portions of our adult social lives. It's an enormous family commitment, but I don't think it was any different than the dedication needed to support a child who's focused on an elite level of any pursuit, be it music, chess, spelling bees, debate, dance, or sports.

We had the advantage of having only two children, so we could split up and manage their sports activities in man-to-man coverage, while families with three or more kids were forced into zone coverage. Large families often brought younger siblings along as tagalongs to practices and games. Despite a reduced focus toward these younger kids at times, the youngsters many times surpassed their older siblings in athletic prowess. Perhaps that was a function of either always playing up against older siblings or their parents better managing the subsequent journeys of these younger kids. Practice makes perfect even for parents managing the journeys.

Since we had only the two kids, Karen and I sometimes assisted those parents in "zone coverage." It's impossible for two parents to attend three or four games scheduled for the same times in different locales. We also had an advantage in that our kids were nearly six years apart in age which separated their peak sport commitments.

A related question we often get is whether our sports journey was worth the financial outlay. I maintained all kinds of records and notes beginning in 2002, which made this book possible, but I never tracked expenses. Karen and I just did not want to know, as we were sure that if we began adding it all up, we'd need medical attention for the shock. That said, I am confident in guesstimating that our family's soccer journey cost well in excess of $50,000 (and our daughter's sports journey in sailing cost much more). We were very fortunate never to have had to equivocate due to costs, but many families are constrained in today's pay-to-play environment [==]. Over the years, we quietly helped out a few financially compromised parents with fees, uniforms, carpooling, and hotel costs.

Our team enjoyed the cost advantages of having many top-level tournaments within daily driving distance (no hotels) and a non-profit sports organization that did not permit coaches to be paid. But because Evan was regularly double-carded, including being rostered on the expensive ODP teams, and participated in more paid supplemental training and sports camps than most peers, those advantages were certainly offset with other expenses.

I suspect even the most frugally managed, elite youth soccer journey would cost a minimum of $25,000 which, sadly, is out of reach for many. If there's a plus to the soccer when it comes to expense, it's that equipment is relatively inexpensive and field access fees are low. Sports like ice hockey, golf, tennis, skiing, and sailing have much higher entry costs. There are ample references to some sports journeys costing as much as $20,000 *per year*, more for a year-round, IMG Academy-type experience. While the high costs, pay-to-play, and non-inclusive aspects of youth sports are well documented and much lamented, the reality is that it costs significant money to support the uniforms, tournaments, leagues, coaching, field time, training, travel, and organizational bureaucracies.

Families may have to commit significant time and money to the youth-sports journey.

Despite the cost to our family in time and money, I can unequivocally answer the question of whether the journey was worth it in one word—*absolutely*! The best evidence of the positive value of sports was that Evan would pop out of the car and instantly be gone to be with his teammates as soon as we arrived at practices or games. His passionate, can't-wait-to-get-back-on-the-field attitude was germane to his journey regardless the team, field, coach, horrible weather, or overhanging homework commitments.

Would I change anything? Certainly. I might have better managed his travel-team selection, especially transitioning to the Fury team or an equivalent team a year earlier. We could have also skipped a few of the big camps if we'd understood what a money churn they were. Despite that issue, Evan probably benefited from the extra training and college connections.

A Game-Changer at the Buzzer

Just when we thought the youth-sports journey was completely through with change, it changed one last time, and this time in a big way.

Change, like the kind I'm about to tell you about, is why college advisors recommend kids select their college based on academics and a comfortable vibe, rather than focusing on the athletic program. Athletic careers can end suddenly due to injury, academic issues, changes of interests, or even a global pandemic. Four months before Evan's freshman year in college was about to begin, he received *the call* from the coach. The coach was moving on. The coach was well-liked by the current players, had promoted excellent team camaraderie, and fostered a playing style that was well-suited to Evan. Evan liked Coach as well, and that was no small thing when it came to the decision to sign with this college.

So much for my thoroughly researched analytics and carefully crafted recommendations I talked about in the earlier chapters. While on the surface this call seemed disastrous, there was nothing to do at this point but wait and see how it turned out. We didn't have a Plan B, but it was too late to put one in motion even if we had one. At least we were able to take comfort in the fact that Evan had selected his college based on his well-researched academic and sports fit.

Three weeks later, Evan received a call from the new head coach. New Coach had been the college's assistant coach at one time before moving on to a bigger program. Now he was back as the head coach, and he got right down to business with Evan by outlining the physical conditioning, summer training, and preseason expectations—and they were perfectly aligned with Evan's focus on fitness. He was still training with the high-level Juventus team, playing against top-thirty teams into the summer after his senior year, and continuing his never-ending supplemental training. He was well prepared for freshman college preseason.

Match Point

Evan's constant supplemental efforts were how this athletically ordinary kid had overcome the many obstacles (including the fifty-four obstacles of Appendix II) to become a recruited college athlete. The key attributes fostering Evan's success, as well that of most of his peers, were perseverance and hard work. I now suspect this grit may be the most critical element of non-gifted, ordinary athletes getting to experience a successful long-term youth journey in any sport. In addition, college athletes benefit from a little targeted marketing (and luck) in connecting to a college coach where they are a good fit. (Evan was no exception, per Appendix III).

> "Persistence can change failure into extraordinary achievement." —Matt Biondi, eleven-time Olympic medalist

Fortunately, Karen and I were an integral part of our son's sports journey, sharing the triumphs and fun moments as well as helping him work through the many challenges. When it comes to an athlete's journey, parents cannot park the bus; they must, at times, be a champion for their athlete. I particularly enjoyed my time riding in the car with Evan, watching his games, advising as a mentor, being a weight-training cohort, and, most especially, being his practice partner for six years. It's not the wins, defensive stops, or assists but rather the relentless perseverance of which I am most proud.

For we parents, coaches and our athletes, and regardless of the endgame; it still should always be about their journey.

Appendices

Appendix I

The Sixteen-Year Sports Journey by the Numbers

1. Day 1 of youth sports—June 23, 2002
2. Day 5,854 of youth sports—July 2, 2018
3. Youth games played since U7—U19
    a. Wins*—387 (54%)
    b. Losses—240 (33%)
    c. Ties—92 (13%)
4. Club (Recreation and travel) Team games played—638
5. High school games played—81
6. League seasons played since U7—51 (4.5 per year)
    a. League season champions*—10 (20%)
    b. League season runners-up—6 (11%)
7. Tournaments played since U7—76 (6.5 per year)
    a. Tournament champions*—8 (11%)
8. Sports camps/clinics attended since U7—44 (4 per year)
9. Coaches since U7—32 (3 per year)

10. Player turnover on primary travel team of 7 years—33 (4.5 per year)
11. Trophies and medals won*—28
12. National team rankings of the two travel teams
    a. Fury: 75-600 (avg. ~ 100)
    b. Juventus: 12-40
13. Maryland state team rankings of the two travel teams
    a. Fury: 5-30 (avg. ~ 8)
    b. Juventus: 2-6
14. Colleges screened—30+
15. Colleges visited (Camps or campus tours)—22
    a. D1—14
    b. D2—0
    c. D3 —8
16. Meetings with Coaches—11
    a. D1—5
    b. D2—0
    c. D3—6
17. College Applications—1

**The travel-team coaches always selected the toughest competition, which favored development over the highest likelihood of winning.*

Appendix II

Fifty-Four Obstacles and Challenges That Youth Athletes Must Overcome (in order of appearance)

1. Select teams and development can begin before age eight, and naïve parents may be late in getting their athletes to the party.
2. Coaches and parents encourage athletes to sub-specialize at the earliest ages. Such an athlete is not only subject to overuse injury, they can be pigeonholed into certain positions without realizing the unintended consequences until later in their athletic careers.
3. Parents and coaches can mistakenly influence (force) their kids to participate in a favored sport or position that may not suit that child's physical characteristics or psyche.
4. Youth-sports organizers may promise athletes an A-level opportunity and then "bait and switch" the athlete to a

B-level to expand those organizational empires, rather than to maximize the potential development of the athlete.

5. A sports parent must constantly find and maintain an appropriate team, level of play, and coach fit for their child.
6. Elite youth sports often become obsessed with and driven by team and player rankings. These rankings can be manipulated in the same manner as sandbagging a golf handicap.
7. The administrative and bureaucratic rules of adult sports organizers, such as carding, rostering, residency, and age requirements, can create barriers to participation and add costs.
8. Unless a sport has definitive performance measures, tryouts and coach selections are, by nature, subjective. Even professionals get draft selections hugely wrong.
9. Coaches selecting on the basis of natural athleticism and size over attributes of skill, tenacity, and work ethic is a never-ending constant in youth sports beginning with the peewee stage.
10. Youth coaches with a laser-like focus on individual player assessments and development are rare. Coaches tend to focus on the overall team and regression of the mean for development needs.
11. Athletes located in the hotbed regions of their chosen sport will have a developmental advantage. Athletes located remotely—think snow skiers in Florida or surfers in Kansas—will require extensive and expensive travel for development and competition.
12. Lack of playing time is perhaps the most prevalent and critical issue in all of youth-sports development, and it begins from the youngest ages. Many coaches manage this issue poorly.

13. Coaches, organizers, and parents often mismanage athletes and teams because of their misguided desire to have their kids win. This overriding objective to win can be witnessed from the earliest ages.
14. Youth players can't be honest with coaches. "Just never, ever give a coach a reason not to play you," is how Evan put it.
15. Sports that switch from a smaller youth roster to a larger roster as children become older will have several years of restructuring athletes, teams and levels of play. In soccer, the switch from eight-versus-eight play (fourteen-player roster) to eleven-versus-eleven play (eighteen-player roster) results in a tumultuous two-year reorganization of teams and players.
16. The different adult-led organizational changes to adult-sized constraints and rules occurred at different ages, which further complicated the re-sorting of athletes, teams, and development.
17. The jump to adult-sized playing constraints (tackling, full-sized fields, checking, full-height hoops and nets, etc.) and rules frequently occurs too early; preteens may not be physically or socially ready to successfully adapt to these changes.
18. Although now standardized, during Evan's journey, the different organizational bureaucracies utilized two age brackets, a calendar year (January to December) and a school year (August to July). This fostered disjointed rosters and teams.
19. When U.S. Soccer standardized the youth calendar-year age brackets in 2017, it did not grandfather in the already established teams above age thirteen. This resulted in a

second two-year tumult of players and teams being re-sorted in the midst of college recruiting for Evan and his peers.

20. Any organization that prohibits or restricts athletes from playing on more or different teams restricts youth development.
21. High school coaches are rightfully restricted from managing athletes outside the school environment. At the same time, other coaches have developed alternative realities of outside teams, camps, and training regimes ("pay here to play there.")
22. While team uniforms are necessary, some adult bureaucracies and team managers have developed over-the-top rules and requirements for these uniforms, creating unnecessary pay-to-play financial barriers.
23. Rules restricting free substitution of youth athletes generally hinder sensible distribution of game time, utilization, and development of players.
24. Ordinary kids (and their parents) must decide and commit to the highest potential level of sports they plan to pursue during the pre-high school years, around ages twelve to thirteen. Failing to do so means the athlete will likely be left behind.
25. Coaches and players should observe how the very best teams practice if they want to improve their own development progress. Such an approach may be more productive than any bureaucratic coaching certification process.
26. Coaches may have an honorable underlying intent but be horrible with kid personnel management, kid communications, and parent and team administrative management.
27. In extreme cases, parent coaches may be all about managing for the benefit of their child, Other athletes may seem

like pawns to assist in the focused development of the coach's child.

28. Parent coaches may not only manage for the benefit of their child, but for their kid's friends. This can foster player clique formation to the detriment of the overall team environment.
29. Coaches who scream, yell, or intimidate never create the ideal youth playing environment.
30. Despite family turmoil, elite youth sports never stop. There may be a short time-out, but they never stop.
31. College recruiting videos take an enormous commitment of time, effort, and money to produce, but many college coaches ignore them.
32. Random field conditions, weather, coach attendance, team performance, a player's physical condition, and a global pandemic can all be critical variables impacting an athlete's future (college) opportunities.
33. Athletes may have to trade off academic and sports standards in their college selection.
34. Many college coaches exhibit an obvious bias for players having specific physical attributes.
35. Some college coaches exhibit an obvious bias in the recruiting and utilization of international players.
36. A few college coaches regularly utilize redshirting, which may not align with a player's desired college experience.
37. Just as in youth sports, college coaches exhibit the complete gamut of player utilization and playing time distribution.
38. Some college coaches exhibit a strong local or regional recruiting bias in sourcing their players.
39. Some college coaches over-recruit. The resulting imbalance creates a four-year issue concerning playing time and team harmony for many players.

40. There are problem coaches everywhere, but unlike with youth play, the ability to change to a better environment may be limited for college athletes.
41. Just as with youth coaches, some college coaches are yellers.
42. Surprisingly, some college coaches foster an unsophisticated team playing style reminiscent of the youth game.
43. Adult organizers scheduling travel-team competitions during and conflicting with school hours is an unadvertised and misguided aspect of youth sports.
44. While the pundit advice is to start college sports recruiting very early on, men's college coaches seem to focus on current-year recruiting. An early start may not benefit boys but may work for girls.
45. Coaches, camp directors, sports organizers, and recruiters regularly mislead (lie to) athletes and parents regarding the likely outcome of the athlete's participation in their activity (camps) because they need paying participants.
46. Many sports camps and related activities regress to the lowest possible means in terms of players attracted and coaching levels that may not provide an adequate training environment for elite athletes.
47. Colleges and coaches may renege on verbal agreements concerning scholarships or roster slots.
48. Both the athlete and the college can incur significant, unanticipated changes as the recruiting and admissions year progresses. Athletes should maintain as much optionality as possible when it comes to committing to a college.
49. The onset of senioritis can negatively impact the final recruiting activities and transition preparations for those athletes progressing toward college sports.
50. Youth sports with large participation numbers provide their athletes with endless opportunities to play and pursue their

dreams at all levels, but these sports also result in daunting competition to get noticed at higher levels, including by college coaches.

51. The likelihood of achieving a college sport roster slot is low (just a few percent for elite high school athletes).
52. The likelihood of receiving even a partial D1 scholarship are dismal.
53. The likelihood of a high school boy playing varsity sports in college is lower than for girls, due to the offsetting (Title IX) exception of large football rosters.
54. Families must manage the time commitment, costs, and the associated pay-to-play environments of youth sports.

Appendix III

What the College Coaches Had to Say

D3 Coach—"I had the pleasure of watching you play a few weekends ago at the Potomac tournament and thought you played very well. You were very comfortable in possession and helped your team build through the midfield to the attacking third. You were also very effective defensively. I thought you screened the back four well and cut off a lot of the opposition's passing lanes. After watching you play at the tournament, we believe that you would be a great fit for us and someone who could make an immediate impact for the program in the fall of 2018."

D3 Coach—"I thought you did very well this weekend and have the ability to help our program. I thought you demonstrated a great work rate defensively and an ability to make good decisions on the ball once you won it."

D1 Coach—"Overall, I thought you showed a great work rate and the ability to elevate your teammates around you. I appreciate your blue-collar mentality to the game."

D3 Coach—"You are a crisp passer of the ball and do a nice role for the team, keeping things moving and playing simple. We believe you are a very good player and have the abilities to be a part of our program. I think you are a very simple player (which is a positive), and you know how to make everyone around you better by making the correct decisions for your team instead of just for yourself. I like the consistency and crispness of your short passing, and I believe you understand the position very well."

D1 Coach—"Evan, I liked how you played as a holding midfielder. Your ability to win tackles really helped your team."

D3 Coach—"Well played! I was able to see you play this weekend at the Jefferson Cup Showcase and liked what I saw!"

D3 Coach—"It was great seeing you play this past weekend at the Jefferson Cup. I thought your Severna Park team did well but I was particularly impressed by you. You operated very well in the middle of the park, and I think you are a player who could help us."

D3 Coach—"As a defensive central midfielder, I liked your work rate and ability to read the game on the defensive side of the ball. I thought that you were a good ball winner and put yourself in good positions to protect your team from counterattacks."

D1 Coach—"In my opinion, one of the things I liked about you as a player was that I felt you were very versatile and comfortable playing in a different number of positions. I also was impressed with how comfortable you were on the ball."

D3 Coach—"I was able to see you play at the Potomac tournament a month ago, and I wanted to reach out to you to let you know I am very interested in you being a part of our program in 2018."

D3 Coach—"I wanted to reach out, as our coaching staff was very impressed with your play at the EDP Showcase this summer. I feel you would be a great fit for our program."

D3 Coach—"I had the opportunity to watch and coach you at the ID camp and was impressed with your overall play as a center midfielder. I liked how you moved on and off the ball, creating good passing lanes or angles to receive or pass a ball. You were simple and composed with the ball at your feet, allowing yourself to play accurate passes to teammates going forward. I also liked how you played the way you were faced and did not try to force it forward if it was not on. Finally, I appreciated how hard you worked on the field. Your work rate was really impressive and will help you out at the next level. It was a pleasure watching you play."

D1 Coach—"You are very calm on the ball and so intelligent in and out of possession."

Appendix IV

Suggested Further Reading

Wetherell, W. D. *Soccer Dad*. Skyhorse Publishing, 2008.

Cruthers, Greg. *Softball Journey*. Self-published, 2021.

Cantwell, Kevin and Pat Alacqua. *Parent's Guide to Youth Basketball and Beyond*. Self-published, 2017.

O'Sullivan, John. *Changing the Game*. Morgan James Publishing, 2014.

Burns, Christie Casciano. *My Kids Play Hockey: Essential Advice for Every Hockey Parent*. Skyhorse Publishing, 2018.

Lewis, Michael. *Playing to Win*. Audible Original, October 2020.

Morris, Steve. *What Size Balls Do I Need?* Self-published, 2020.

Abdou, Angie. *Home Ice: Reflections of a Reluctant Hockey Mom*. ECW Press, 2018.

Hyman, Mark. *The Most Expensive Game in Town*. Beacon Press, 2013.

Lynch, Jerry. *Let Them Play*. New World Library, 2016.

Hyman, Mark. *Until it Hurts*. Beacon Press, 2009.

Farrey, Tom. *Game On; The All-American Race to Make Champions of Our Children.* ESPN, 2008. Director of *Project Play* at The Aspen Institute: www.aspenprojectplay.org

Just, Mike. *Just Baseball: A Guide to Navigating the World of Baseball Recruitment for Players and Parents.* Skyhorse Publishing, 2017.

Afremow, Jim. *The Champion's Mind.* Rodale Inc, 2013.

Cohen, Rich. *Pee Wees: Confessions of a Hockey Parent.* Farrrar, Straus and Giroux, 2021.

Zartman, Sharkie and Dr. Robert Weil. *#HeySportsParents: An Essential Guide for any Parent with a Child in Sports.* Spoilers Press, 2018

Wolff, Rick. *The Sports Parenting Edge.* Running Press, 2003.

Bigelow, Bob, Tom Moroney and Linda Hall. *Just Let the Kids Play.* Health Communications Publications, 2001.

Engh, Fred. *Why Johnny Hates Sports.* Avery, 1999.

Taylor, Jim. *Raising Young Athletes.* Rowman & Littlefield, 2018.

Bibliography and Quote Sources

Bigelow, Bob, Tom Moroney, and Linda Hall. *Just Let the Kids Play*. Deerfield Beach: Health Communications Publications, 2001. Page 113.

Biondi, Matt—azquotes.com/quote/537297

Bird, Larry—azquotes.com/quote/553244

Cirvoski, Sasho. *Fuel Soccer*. U.S. Soccer. Summer 2019. fuel.usyouthsoccer.org/a-guide-to-tryouts-love-the-game-first/

Cohen, Rich. *Pee Wees: Confessions of a Hockey Parent*. Farrar, Straus and Giroux, 2021. Page 131.

Dolan, Pat. *USA Today*. May 27, 2016.—usatodayhss.com/2016/recruiting-column-3-quotes-that-will-change-your-recruiting-life

Dorrance, Anson—azquotes.com/quote/753090

Engh, Fred. *Why Johnny Hates Sports*. Garden City Park: Avery Publishing Group, 1999. Page 82.

Gladwell, Malcolm. *Outliers*. New York: Little, Brown and Company, 2008.

Goldberg, Dr. Alan. "Hey Coach, What's Wrong with You?" August 15, 2015. competitivedge.com/hey-coach-whats-wrong-with-you/

Gretzky, Wayne—brainyquote.com/quotes/wayne_gretzky_131510

Matheny, Mike. *Matheny Manifesto*. 2009. cdn1.sportngin.com/attachments/document/3ae2-1690134/Matheny_Manifesto_-_Letter_to_Parents_-_Character_Development.pdf

NCAA—www.ncaa.com/

O'Sullivan, John. "The Enemy of Excellence in Youth Sports." Changing the Game Project, January 8, 2015. changingthegameproject.com/the-enemy-of-excellence-in-youth-sports/

Pulisic, Christian. "1,834 Days". Players Tribune, November 13, 2017.theplayerstribune.com/en-us/articles/christian-pulisic-usmnt-world-cup

Scholarshipstats.com

Sports and Fitness Industry Association—https://www.sfia.org/andengagesports.com/blog/post/1488/youth-sports-participation-statistics-and-trends

Squawka.com—squawka.com/en/

Summitt, Pat—azquotes.com/quote/761698

Thompson, Derek. "The Cult of Rich Kids Sports," *The Atlantic*, October 2, 2019.

Wolff, Rick. *The Sports Parenting Edge*. Philadelphia: Running Press, 2003. Page 95.

Wooden, John—goodreads.com/quotes/8592114-a-good-coach-can-change-a-game-a-great-coach